VATICAN II
AT 60

VATICAN II AT 60

Re-Energizing the Renewal

Edited by Catherine E. Clifford
with Stephen Lampe

Maryknoll, New York 10545

The publishing arm of the Maryknoll Fathers and Brothers, Orbis seeks to explore the global dimensions of the Christian faith and mission, to invite dialogue with diverse cultures and religious traditions, and to serve the cause of reconciliation and peace. The books published reflect the views of their authors and do not represent the official position of the Maryknoll Society. To learn more about Maryknoll and Orbis Books, please visit our website at www.orbisbooks.com.

Published by Orbis Books, Box 302, Maryknoll, NY 10545-0302.

Manufactured in the United States of America

Library of Congress Cataloging-in-Publication Data

Names: Clifford, Catherine E., 1958- editor. | Lampe, Stephen (Stephen J.), editor.
Title: Vatican II at 60 : re-energizing the renewal / edited by Catherine Clifford with Stephen Lampe.
Other titles: Vatican two at sixty : re-energizing the renewal
Description: Maryknoll, NY : Orbis Books, [2024] | Includes bibliographical references. | Contents: A council that will never end : the unfinished business of Lumen gentium / Paul Lakeland—Nostra aetate : journey to interfaith dialogue / Celia Deutsch, NDS—Synodality : an enduring legacy of the council / Cardinal Robert W. McElroy.
Identifiers: LCCN 2023044948 (print) | LCCN 2023044949 (ebook) | ISBN 9781626985575 (trade paperback) | ISBN 9798888660157 (epub)
Subjects: LCSH: Vatican Council (2nd : 1962-1965 : Basilica di San Pietro in Vaticano)
Classification: LCC BX830 1962 .V3217 2024 (print) | LCC BX830 1962 (ebook) | DDC 262/.52—dc23/eng/20231127
LC record available at https://lccn.loc.gov/2023044948
LC ebook record available at https://lccn.loc.gov/2023044949

Contents

Foreword and Acknowledgments

The essays in this volume began as presentations for *Re-Energizing the Renewal: A Webinar Series to Celebrate the 60th Anniversary of the Second Vatican Council*. That council, which opened on October 11, 1962, and closed on December 8, 1965, was a watershed moment in the history of the Catholic Church. During four sessions held from 1962 to 1965, topics essential to the life of the Catholic Church and its relationship to the modern world, to other Christians, and to other religious traditions were raised and debated. As a result of those deliberations the council produced sixteen documents that have guided the church over the past sixty years and continue to shape it.

The series was conceived and sponsored by *Spirit Alive: The CSJ Institute for Faith Inquiry and Education*, a ministry of the Sisters of Saint Joseph, Brentwood, New York, to showcase the teaching and spirit of the council's major documents and themes and consider their relevance for our own day. Each member of the Spirit Alive advisory board, still animated by the vision set forth at the council, agreed that we could not let the occasion of Vatican II's sixtieth anniversary pass without providing an opportunity for both young and old to (re)consider and be (re)energized by the council's vision of the church and its mission in our world.

Neither the webinar series nor this volume could have

been possible without the support of many people. My thanks go first to Paul Lakeland. When I approached him with the idea for this program, he was enthusiastic, offered to do the first presentation, and gave invaluable advice on shaping the series. I am also grateful to each of the contributors. Though all busy academics and prelates, each responded enthusiastically to the invitation to do a webinar presentation and then submit it for publication. I also owe a word of thanks to two very important behind-the-scenes persons: Matthew Mobijohn, our Spirit Alive IT tech, and Kim Mailley, who handles all the organizational work and communication for me.

When Robert Ellsberg expressed his interest in publishing this volume, Catherine Clifford graciously stepped forward to edit the submissions. I am immensely grateful to Catherine and to Stephen Lampe, a priest of the Milwaukee Archdiocese and a Spirit Alive advisory board member, who assisted her in all the detailed and labor-intensive work needed to bring this volume to fruition.

I am grateful also to the many people who wrote to me, thanking Spirit Alive for the Vatican II series that revived their hope in and for the church. More than a few recalled how the ecclesial vision of Vatican II had inspired them to drop their nets and put their lives at the service of the people of God whether as priests, religious, or lay ecclesial ministers. They also acknowledged that together we have an obligation to do all we can to continue the renewal and reform inaugurated by the council lest that vision pass from experience and memory into history.

Finally, I would like to express my thanks to Sister Tesa Fitzgerald, CSJ, president of the Sisters of Saint Joseph, and all the members of my congregation who enthusiastically support Spirit Alive's mission. Along with many generous benefactors, and a generous grant from the Raskob Foundation, the congregation has graciously provided the financial support needed for our programming. Thanks to this generosity, and to technology, we have been able to go beyond classroom buildings to extend the educational ministry that our congregation has embraced for over 150 years and continue our work of passing on the faith and keeping the Spirit alive!

Maria Pascuzzi, CSJ, SSL, STD
Director, Spirit Alive
October 11, 2023—Feast of Pope Saint John XXIII

Abbreviations

Citations from the documents of Vatican II, from *Vatican Council II: Constitutions, Decrees, Declarations. The Basic Sixteen Documents*. Edited by Austin Flannery, OP © 1996 (Collegeville, MN: Liturgical Press, 2014). Used with permission.

- **AA** *Apostolicam Actuositatem*, Decree on the Apostolate of Lay People, November 8, 1965
- **AG** *Ad Gentes*, Decree on the Church's Missionary Activity, December 7, 1965
- **CD** *Christus Dominus*, Decree on the Pastoral Office of Bishops in the Church, October 28, 1965
- **DH** *Dignitatis Humanae*, Declaration on Religious Liberty, December 7, 1965
- **DV** *Dei Verbum*, Dogmatic Constitution on Divine Revelation, November 18, 1965
- **GE** *Gravissimum Educationis*, Declaration on Christian Education, October 28, 1965
- **GS** *Gaudium et Spes*, Pastoral Constitution on the Church in the Modern World, December 7, 1965
- **IM** *Inter Mirifica*, Decree on the Mass Media, December 4, 1963
- **LG** *Lumen Gentium*, Dogmatic Constitution on the Church, November 21, 1964
- **NA** *Nostra Aetate*, Declaration on the Relation of the Church to Non-Christian Religions, October 28, 1965

OE	*Orientalium Ecclesiarum*, Decree on the Catholic Eastern Churches, November 21, 1964
OT	*Optatam Totius*, Decree on the Training of Priests, October 28, 1965
PC	*Perfectae Caritatis*, Decree on the Up-to-Date Renewal of Religious Life, October 28, 1965
PO	*Presbyterorum Ordinis*, Decree on the Ministry and Life of Priests, December 7, 1965
SC	*Sacrosanctum Concilium*, Constitution on the Sacred Liturgy, December 4, 1963
UR	*Unitatis Redintegratio*, Decree on Ecumenism, November 21, 1964

Contributors

John F. Baldovin, SJ, is Professor of Historical and Liturgical Theology at the Boston College School of Theology and Ministry. He is the author of *Reforming the Liturgy: A Response to the Critics* (2008).

Catherine E. Clifford is Professor of Systematic and Historical Theology at Saint Paul University, Ottawa. She is coeditor, with Massimo Faggioli, of *The Oxford Handbook on Vatican II* (2023).

Cardinal Blase J. Cupich is the Archbishop of the Archdiocese of Chicago.

Celia Deutsch, NDS, is Research Scholar in the Religion Department at Barnard College. She has written extensively in the fields of early Judaism and Christianity, as well as Jewish-Christian relations.

Brian P. Flanagan is Senior Fellow at New Ways Ministry, working to connect theologians and scholars with New Ways Ministry's work for equity, inclusion, and justice for LGBTQ+ persons in the Catholic Church. He is the author of *Stumbling into Holiness: Sin and Sanctity in the Church* (2018).

Paul Lakeland is Professor Emeritus and Founding Director of the Center for Catholic Studies at Fairfield University,

Connecticut. He is the author of many books, most recently, *The Wounded Angel: Fiction and the Religious Imagination* (2017).

Cardinal Robert W. McElroy is Bishop of the Diocese of San Diego. He has written *The Search for an American Public Theology: The Contribution of John Courtney Murray* (1989) and *Morality and American Foreign Policy* (2016).

Marcus Mescher is Associate Professor of Christian Ethics at Xavier University, Cincinnati, Ohio, specializing in Catholic Social Thought and Moral Formation. He has published *The Ethics of Encounter: Christian Neighbor Love as a Practice of Solidarity* (2020).

Gerald O'Collins, SJ, was most recently Research Professor and Writer-in-Residence at the Jesuit Theological College in Parkville, Victoria, Australia, following a long and distinguished career. He has authored over eighty books, including the award-winning *Living Vatican II: The 21st-Century Council for the 21st Century* (2006).

Elyse J. Raby is Assistant Professor in the Department of Religious Studies at Santa Clara University. She has published on questions relating to ecclesiology, embodiment, and gender.

Ormond Rush is currently Associate Professor and Reader at Australian Catholic University, Brisbane campus. His publications include *The Eyes of Faith: The Sense of the Faithful and the Church's Reception of Revelation* (2009) and *The Vision of Vatican II: Its Fundamental Principles* (2019).

Preface

Cardinal Blaise J. Cupich

Twenty-one times in the church's nearly two-thousand-year history, universal (or ecumenical) councils have been held, identified by such iconic names as Nicaea, Chalcedon, Ephesus, Trent, and Vatican I, to name just a few. These councils were called to assist the church in specific ages (and future generations as well), to remain faithful to its tradition and to navigate the challenges of its particular age. Such councils did not happen by accident. Rather, they responded to specific challenges, whether the challenge was to more clearly define, or even correct, a central teaching of the faith, or to reform and renew the church in troubled social and political times. Two aspects were constant. First, the church, as a living and dynamic community, called such universal councils to preserve and correctly understand its tradition, and to face the unforeseen challenges of ever-changing social and political contexts. Second, though each council already began to shape the church and its tradition in its time, the process of appropriating the teachings of each council required decades of reflection as the council's insights slowly became part of the fabric of the church.[1]

---

[1] "The crucial process of reception, that all-important part of any church council, which can take several generations, had begun. It continues today." Cardinal Franz König, "It Must Be the Holy Spirit," *The Tablet* December 21, 2002.

Fifty-seven years have passed since the most recent ecumenical council, popularly known as Vatican II. First convened on October 11, 1962, and concluded on December 8, 1965, the council produced a total of sixteen documents: four constitutions, nine decrees, and three declarations. In 2012, on the fiftieth anniversary of Vatican II, Pope Emeritus Benedict XVI indicated that it was to be a council of renewal when he wrote that "Christianity, which had built and formed the Western world, seemed more and more to be losing its power to shape society. It appeared weary and it looked as if the future would be determined by other spiritual forces. The sense of this loss of the present on the part of Christianity, and of the task following on from that, was well summed up in the word '*aggiornamento*' (updating). Christianity must be in the present if it is to be able to form the future."[2] If *aggiornamento* was the goal, the council strove to remain rooted in its ancient tradition by following the principle called *ressourcement*, which sought insight by going back to the sources: the biblical text, the earliest forms of the liturgy, the early church councils, and the writings of the fathers of the church.

Church historian and theologian Fr. John O'Malley wrote that Vatican II was "the most important religious event of the twentieth century,"[3] and religious leaders of

---

[2] Benedict XVI, "Reflections of His Holiness Benedict XVI Published for the First Time on the Occasion of the 50th Anniversary of the Opening of the Second Vatican Council," August 2, 2012. Fr. Gerald O'Collins says much the same when he writes, "Pope John hoped that this assembly of Roman Catholic bishops, joined by observers from other Christian churches and communities, would bring about a new Pentecost. He wanted to update and renew spiritually the Catholic Church, heal divisions within Christendom, and alter the Church's reactionary attitude toward the world." Gerald O'Collins, *The Second Vatican Council: Message and Meaning* (Collegeville, MN: Liturgical Press, 2014), vii.

[3] John W. O'Malley, *What Happened at Vatican II?* (Cambridge, MA: Belknap Press of Harvard University Press, 2008), 1.

many different faiths concurred. For average Catholics, the most evident effects were the changes experienced in the liturgy and in their daily experience of parish life. For bishops, priests, and religious, the council not only affected their liturgical lives but also their self-understanding. With calls to retrieve the original charism of their religious orders and institutes, religious communities of men and women experienced enormous change. As with all councils, some of these changes were welcomed, even as others were resisted, or even rejected. In the past fifty-seven years, the council has been praised and blamed. Some have already called for a third Vatican council, others would like to nullify Vatican II as a misbegotten concession to the modern world, and still others call for a reform of the reform.

In the light of such natural tensions, it bears remembering that it takes decades for a council to be received. The same is true with Vatican II. Just as each council forms part of our precious tradition, so too the documents of Vatican II have become an indispensable part of that very same tradition. For those who are calling for a return to the tradition, that is exactly what we need. But what I mean is that it is time for us to reread the documents of Vatican II (or perhaps to read them for the first time), as these documents are a precious and insightful contribution to the church's teaching and tradition.[4] It is time to reread these inspired docu-

[4] Massimo Faggioli makes this point powerfully when he writes, "Vatican II needs an interpretation that speaks to the receivers of that tradition *today*. We can't ask Pope Francis to do it alone while we let his opponents aggressively work to abrogate it. Simply countering or reacting to right-wing traditionalists isn't a defense; it just won't work. Rather, it's time to take up the theological meaning of the documents of Vatican II and the magisterial significance of the conciliar event. The Catholic Church is called to begin again, especially in the United States—in the seminaries, in the parishes, in academia—to undertake a process of the reception of the theology of Vatican II that puts aside generational rifts and fills the gaps in

ments from the largest assembly of Catholic bishops and other religious observers that has ever been assembled for an ecumenical council. It is time to read (or reread) these documents not only for their message but also for their dynamism, realizing that they are the tradition of a living church that needs their message and dynamism as much today as it did in 1965. In the preface to his 2014 book, *The Second Vatican Council: Message and Meaning*, the Jesuit Fr. Gerald O'Collins wrote, "Understanding, interpreting, and implementing Vatican II's texts remain a still far-from-completed task. . . . The documents can still astonish me with the golden bits. Much of what the Council taught remains to be appreciated and practiced."[5] The time has surely come to collect those "golden bits," to appreciate this precious part of our tradition, and to practice its timeless lessons and teachings in our time.

As Pope Francis underscores in the preface to *Siblings All, Sign of the Times*, the recently released book on his contributions to Catholic social teaching, it is necessary to make more explicit the key concepts of the Second Vatican Council, the foundations of its arguments, its theological and pastoral horizon, the arguments, and the method it used.[6]

I want to offer my special thanks to the Sisters of St. Joseph of Brentwood, New York, for offering this series to commemorate the sixtieth anniversary of the Second Vatican Council. I am confident that you will benefit from it. God bless you all!

---

conciliar teaching. We can do that by building on the very basis of the *tradition* dynamically understood, as opposed to 'tradition' that emphasizes contrast, conflict, and conquest." Massimo Faggioli, "The Limits of '*Traditionis Custodes*,'" *Commonweal*, September 2, 2021.

[5] O'Collins, *Message and Meaning*, ix.

[6] Michael Czerny and Christian Barone, *Siblings All, Sign of the Times: The Social Teaching of Pope Francis*, trans. Julian Paparella (Maryknoll, NY: Orbis Books, 2022), ix–xiv.

Introduction

Catherine E. Clifford

One might be forgiven for not noticing that we are now sixty years from the historic meeting of the Second Vatican Council (1962–1965). We entered this anniversary period during a global pandemic, a global climate crisis, a crisis of migration, an outbreak of war on the European continent with global repercussions, not to mention the internal crises affecting the life of the church. We owe a debt of gratitude to the Sisters of St. Joseph of Brentwood, New York, for taking the initiative to organize this lecture series, "Re-Energizing the Renewal," helping us to keep our eye on the ball, so to speak, and not letting the clamor all around us take our focus from an attentive listening to God's Spirit. The sixtieth anniversary of the Second Vatican Council falls at a critical moment, when Catholics and other Christians urgently reflect on what is being asked of the church in our time. Vatican II remains a sure guide for its life and mission as we confront new questions and navigate new challenges.

Much attention is now focused on the Synod on Synodality (2021–2024)—a process rooted in the vision of Vatican II and aimed at mobilizing the energies of Catholics at every level of the global church, at learning to become a more synodal, participatory church. It seeks to free up the energies of all the baptized to witness and proclaim the Gospel. At the same time, preparations are quietly underway to celebrate a Jubilee Year in 2025 with the theme "Pilgrims in Hope." The year 2025 marks the seventeenth centenary of the first ecumenical council, the Council of Nicaea, a synodal event that gathered representatives of the whole Christian community in the fourth century to clarify our understanding of Jesus as the Son of God and Incarnate Word, the revelation of God's love for all humanity. We continue to profess the faith that has been handed down from those early Christians each time we recite the Nicene Creed and enflesh its message in works of mercy.

It has been suggested that the best preparation for this renewal of the pilgrim people of God is a careful rereading of the documents of the Second Vatican Council, with particular attention to the four constitutions: the Constitution on Sacred Liturgy (*Sacrosanctum Concilium*), the Dogmatic Constitution on the Church (*Lumen Gentium*), the Dogmatic Constitution on Divine Revelation (*Dei Verbum*), and the Pastoral Constitution on the Church in the Modern World (*Gaudium et Spes*). This volume provides a solid introduction to those texts. Chapters dedicated to the various council documents help us to understand the context of their elaboration, their central teachings, and the challenge of receiving them today, of letting their insights more fully inform the life and practice of the church. They also recognize the limits of the council's teaching and the need for fresh thinking in the face of new and unforeseen challenges.

Chapters 1 and 2 lay out the context of the Second Vatican Council. In the first, I attempt to show how the task facing the church on the eve of the council, as today, was to find a way of teaching and witnessing to the Gospel that would speak to contemporary people, of acknowledging the movements of God's Spirit in the world, and of bringing a message of hope to those in need. The insight of the German Jesuit Karl Rahner concerning the coming of age of a "world church" at Vatican II provides a lens for understanding the deepening consciousness of the global Catholic community of the need for a more profound integration of faith with the riches of every culture. Though we inhabit a very different world today, the council's teaching and way of proceeding continue to guide and inspire us. Paul Lakeland reflects on how Vatican II's teaching was marked by the contributions of four exemplary theologians (Bernard Lonergan, SJ; Karl Rahner, SJ; Yves Congar, OP; John Courtney Murray, SJ). Insights that matured in movements of biblical, liturgical, and theological renewal were received into official Catholic teaching. The sixteen council documents are informed by a deeper sense of historicity; a return to the early sources of the life and prayer of the church; a fresh understanding of the dignity of each person created in the image of God, who speaks in the depths of every conscience; and a renewed appreciation of the universality of God's offer of saving grace. As Lakeland contends, these developments were hard-won in the anti-Modernist climate that reigned in the early twentieth century and in the lively confrontation of ideas that ensued in the conciliar debate. Not surprisingly, their reception has been neither easy nor unmitigated.

Chapters 3 to 6 treat the four constitutions of Vatican II and their importance today. John Baldovin, SJ, reflects on the first document promulgated by the council, the Constitution on the Liturgy. Essentially a charter for reform, its principles guided the revision of the Roman Rite of the sacraments and the development of new lectionaries for Sundays and weekdays. Baldovin shows how closely these principles of the liturgy—an action of the gathered people of God—are related to the council's ecclesiology. In chapter 4 Brian Flanagan reflects on how the Dogmatic Constitution on the Church's renewed understanding of the dignity and equality of all the baptized is still being received as we seek to re-enliven the church in synodal styles of leadership and structures for participation and shared decision-making and discernment. While the documents of Vatican

II never use the word "synodality," the council itself was a synodal gathering, an event that gave us a foretaste of the dynamic synergy that is possible when the people of God come together and place all their gifts at the service of God's mission. In chapter 5 Ormond Rush explores the dynamic and synodal way the church receives God's self-revelation in his consideration of the Dogmatic Constitution on Divine Revelation. He aptly shows how God continues to speak and we grow in understanding whenever that revelation is re-received through the dynamic interaction of the baptized faithful, theologians, and bishops. In chapter 6 Marcus Mescher considers the strengths and limits of the Pastoral Constitution on the Church in the Modern World, the first conciliar document in the history of the church addressed to all people of goodwill. He shows how its teaching continues to influence the search for a church in solidarity with all, especially with the poor, and open to fraternal collaboration with people of all religions and no religion in service of a world that is more just.

Chapters 7 to 10 explore some of the challenges of receiving the council's teaching in the present. Elyse J. Raby looks in chapter 7 at the council's recognition of the dignity and equality of women and the continuing task, despite important progress, of integrating the gifts of women and of differently gendered persons more fully into the life of the church. In chapter 8 Celia Deutsch, NDS, revisits the council's historic recognition of all that is good and true in other religions and its categorical rejection of all forms of anti-Semitism, underlining the values of dialogue and collaboration that are sorely needed in the polarized context of our day. In chapter 9 Gerald O'Collins, SJ, reflects on the council's teaching as a resource for a spirituality that is Christ-centered, nourished by the Word of God and by our participation in the paschal mystery through the liturgy.

A final chapter by Cardinal Robert McElroy shows how the synod and synodality, and Pope Francis's conviction that synodality is "what God expects of the church in the third millennium," are deeply rooted in the teaching of the Second Vatican Council. Indeed, the synodal process now underway, the fruits of which Cardinal McElroy helpfully summarizes, is to be seen as a new stage in the reception of the council's teaching.

I am most grateful to all our contributors for their passionate and engaging reflections. They help to show how the teaching and the experience of the Second Vatican Council remain a vital touchstone for understanding the nature and mission of the church. Thanks as well to Stephen Lampe for his generous assistance in the preparation of this monograph. May it serve as a rich and informative resource for readers and help to re-energize the forces of renewal at work in the church today.

1

A Council for a World Church

Catherine E. Clifford

The Second Vatican Council, a historic meeting of the world's Catholic bishops from 1962 to 1965—which set a course for the renewal of the Catholic Church and its mission in the modern world and shaped the ecclesial imagination of those who lived through it—is a world away from that of young Christians and contemporary seekers. Sixty years later they rightly ask, can a church council called to respond to the challenges facing the church in the mid-twentieth century still speak to the church and world of the twenty-first? To respond to this concern, one must first ask, "What is a council?" We must also consider the defining features of the world context in the 1960s and how they compare with the context of today's world. Finally, I suggest several ways that Pope Francis is building on the foundations laid by Vatican II to help us realize more fully its vision for a world church, one that carries forward the perennial mission of proclaiming the hope of the Gospel to all.

In the course of this essay, I draw from the interpretation of the German theologian Karl Rahner (1904–1984), who served as an expert adviser to the bishops during the council, especially his contention that at Vatican II we witnessed the "first official" assertion of a church more deeply aware of itself as a "world church."[1] Rahner's theological insight gives us a framework for understanding the continuing evolution of the church in this new millennium, as the global Catholic Church is called to meet the complex task of becoming more fully inculturated. The council's teaching reflects a new awareness of both the changing social location of the church in the modern world and of the permanent dialectic between faith and culture that remains the "law" of evangelization (GS 44), a dynamic that demands a more intentional and responsible engagement in our time.

What Is a Council?

In the long history of the church, the gathered community of God's covenant in Jesus Christ has come together to listen, to pray, to discern, and to deliberate whenever it is confronted with new challenges. In the earliest account of such a gathering, recorded in chapter 15 of the Acts of the Apostles, we find the early Christian community gathered in Jerusalem to resolve a conflict concerning the necessity of following the prescriptions of the Jewish Law,

---

[1] Karl Rahner, "Towards a Fundamental Theological Interpretation of the Second Vatican Council," trans. Leo O'Donovan, *Theological Studies* 40 (1979): 716–27, at 717. This text was initially delivered as a public lecture at an academic convocation at the Weston School of Theology, April 8, 1979, Cambridge, MA. For a fuller version, see the German original in *Das Zweite Vatikanum. Beiträge zum Konzil und seiner Interpretation,* ed. Günther Wassilowsky, 2 vols. (Freiburg: Herder, 2013–2014), 2:958–81; see also "Basic Theological Interpretation of the Second Vatican Council," and "The Abiding Significance of the Second Vatican Council," in *Theological Investigations,* vol. 20, *Concern for the Church,* trans. Edward Quinn (New York: Crossroad, 1981), 77–89, at 78, and 90–102.

in particular the practice of circumcision, to receive the gift of salvation in Jesus Christ. This account reflects a conflict between Jewish Christians and Christians of Greek and other cultural origins in the first century. Apostles and elders gathered to listen to the experience of Paul and Barnabas of what God was accomplishing among the Gentiles, how God was forming "a people for his name" (Acts 15:14), one that transcended the ethnic boundaries of the people of Israel. They acted "with the consent of the whole church" and sent word to the Gentile community to affirm the work of God's Spirit among them and to share their decision to refrain from imposing unnecessary burdens on non-Jewish converts to faith in Christ (Acts 15:22–29).

The most solemn exercise of the teaching office of the bishops acting in concert with the bishop of Rome is found in the gathering of an ecumenical council. Their consensus symbolizes and expresses the communion of faith among the local churches. That unity in faith is both synchronic—reflected by the consensus of the churches gathered from every corner of the world—and diachronic, as the meaning of the apostolic faith discerned at a decisive moment in the past endures and is carried forward within a living tradition. It goes without saying that every council and its teachings are shaped by a host of historical, social, and cultural factors that condition both its agenda and chosen modes of proclamation.

When, during the Week of Prayer for Christian Unity in 1959, Pope John XXIII declared his intention to call a general council of the Catholic Church, he identified two rather traditional aims: first, to bring the church up to date (*aggiornamento*)—a form of church reform; and second, to further the cause of reconciliation between the separated churches—a call to unity in faith.[2] At the time, few saw any

---

[2] The original Italian text of Pope John's speech referred to a "general council." He was surely aware that divisions among the

pressing doctrinal conflict that required resolution. In his official letter convoking the council on Christmas Day 1961, Pope John noted "a crisis underway in human society."[3] "Humanity," he said, "is on the edge of a new era," one that called for a new response on the part of the church if it hoped to bring the light of the Gospel to bear. It was this "sense of responsibility," born from his reading of the "signs of the times" (Matt 16:1–4) that impelled him to call for a substantial reform of the church. Among those signs of God's Spirit at work, he noted a deepening awareness of the dignity of the human person, a desire—following the devastation of two world wars—for peace and stability among the nations, and in the recent establishment of the World Council of Churches (1948), a new effort to foster visible ecclesial unity.

In his historic speech at the opening of the council's first session on October 11, 1962, Pope John was unequivocal.[4] The purpose of the council was not to set aside the tradition nor depart from the truth of the Gospel. Nonetheless, because the world was changing, the ways of proclaiming it must be brought up to date and adapted to the present context. What was needed, he insisted, was that the sure doctrine of the church be "investigated and presented in the way demanded by our times," and using the best of modern

---

Christian churches made it impossible to hold a truly "ecumenical" council—one that would express the faith of all Christians throughout the world. The published version was revised by curial officials ("un Sinodo Diocesano per l'Urbe, e . . . un Concilio Ecumenico per la Chiesa universale"). *Acta Apostolicae Sedis* 51 (1959): 65–69, at 68.

[3] John XXIII, "Pope John Convokes the Second Vatican Council" [*Humanae Salutis*], in *Council Daybook: Vatican II*, vol. 1, *Session 1 (Oct. 11 to Dec. 8, 1962)* and *Session 2 (Sept. 29 to Dec. 4, 1963)*, ed. Floyd Anderson (Washington, DC: National Catholic Welfare Conference, 1965), 1:6–9, at 6.

[4] John XXIII, "Pope John's Opening Speech" [*Gaudet Mater Ecclesia*], in *Council Daybook*, 1:25–29.

methods. He distinguished carefully between the "deposit of faith" or the enduring truths of Christian doctrine and "the way they are expressed." New ways of speaking, of being church, and of witnessing to the faith, he argued, would require "a great deal of work" and "patience." Pope John referred to this as the "pastoral character" of the council's teaching, calling the bishops to proclaim the Gospel with greater effect. The salient feature of their teaching would be in the effort to speak to contemporary people in a language and in forms better adapted to those who might receive it.

The initial preparatory phase of the council did not go particularly well. Many members of the Roman Curia and theologians of the Roman universities largely controlled the agenda, preparing over seventy draft documents in advance of the bishops' gathering. They were not so forward looking. Instead, they saw the council as an opportunity to repeat and now elevate the teachings of the nineteenth- and twentieth-century popes, to endow them with the weight of conciliar authority. In response, Pope John argued that it would be insufficient merely to restate more forcefully or "repeat at length what the fathers and the ancient or more recent theologians have handed on." An ecumenical council would not be needed for this. The more important task before them was to proclaim the Gospel to a different world, to societies and cultures that had radically changed and continue to evolve at an accelerating pace.

Karl Rahner, who provided significant theological advice to Cardinal Franz König of Vienna concerning the documents emerging from the preparatory phase of the council, argued that the council must not only look back at the accumulation of magisterial teaching, but that it must attend to the charismatic gifts of the Holy Spirit at work in the life of the church.[5] These charisms or spiritual gifts are not

---

[5] Karl Rahner, *The Dynamic Element in the Church* (Quaestiones Disputatae), vol. 12, trans. W. J. O'Hara (Freiburg: Herder, 1964).

given to the ordained alone, but reside with all the baptized faithful who are called to discern the call of God and take initiative in the world—not simply carrying out the orders of the hierarchy. Indeed, Rahner observed, the gifts and guidance of the Spirit imply at times a burden, and even a measure of suffering, born out of the dissonance and even opposition to immobility and fixed ways of proceeding.

The council would affirm the charismatic nature of the whole church as a Spirit-led community when, in the Dogmatic Constitution on the Church (*Lumen Gentium*), it recalled the prophetic character of all those anointed by the Spirit at baptism and reflected in the sense of the faithful (*sensus fidei*), their innate capacity for discerning the truth of the Gospel (LG 12). The consensus of the whole church, from the bishops down to the last of the faithful, is a sign and confirmation of the guidance of the Spirit, whom Jesus promised would continue to teach and recall all that he had confided to his disciples (John 14:26). For Rahner, this same Spirit was guiding the whole church in its discernment of the presence and action of the Spirit not only in the church but in the world, in what Pope John was calling the "signs of the time."

The World of Vatican II

What kind of world was this? Fewer than twenty years had transpired since the end of the Second World War. In the wake of the systematic extermination of six million Jews under the Nazi regime, Christian leaders were now challenged to confront the distorting influence of anti-Semitism in Christian preaching and practice. It was the height of the Cold War between the Western alliance and the Soviet Union. The Cuban missile crisis broke out during the first week of council proceedings when, following the discovery of Soviet nuclear weapons deployed on the island of Cuba and aimed at major population centers across North

America, President Kennedy announced a military blockade. The growing influence of communist regimes reflected the increasing sway of atheism. A new age of global communications was dawning thanks to the development of new satellite technology. The chastening of European powers in the wars of the twentieth century brought an end to direct colonial rule. Between 1945 and 1975, at least seventy-five countries in Asia and Africa would gain their independence.

The world—especially the non-European world with its diversity of cultures, the non-Roman church and the diversity of ecclesial communions, the non-Christian world, and the fact of religious pluralism—would be the touchstone of the council's reflection by a church whose reach now extended to the ends of the earth. The French Dominican Yves Congar, who had been named as a consulter to the council's preparatory theological commission, submitted a remarkable note in response to John XXIII's consultation on the conciliar agenda. Lamenting that the questions being considered by that commission resembled more closely those of the First Vatican Council than Pope John's concerns, he ventured,

> Everywhere, but especially among Catholic lay people, the announcement of the Second Vatican Council has aroused great interest and great hope, above all because His Holiness has given promoting the re-establishment of unity among Christians as the Council's distant goal. For churchmen, this interest and this hope constitute a great Christian responsibility before the world.
>
> What world?
>
> A world in which one person in four is Chinese.
>
> A world in which one person in three lives under a Communist regime.
>
> A world in which Christians are divided, but where there is also ecumenical hope.
>
> A world of practical atheism in an immense number

> of people; a world of technology and of an almost general conviction among the young that human beings have the power, thanks to this technology, to organize human life rationally and successfully, by themselves.
>
> A world which denounces Colonialism and any sort of Paternalism.
>
> A world in which women are advancing.
>
> To my mind, all the work of the Council should be undertaken as if under the eyes of *this very* world, as if it were watching us, and with consideration of the realities I have just too briefly evoked.[6]

It was this world that Vatican II sought to address, and this context to which the church would need to adapt its ways of proclamation and witness. Since the French Revolution, Catholicism had largely styled itself as a wounded yet morally superior force, a closed parallel society that stood in judgment over and against a hostile and increasingly secular modern world. In many sectors, its anti-Modern zeal had so turned in upon itself that the church had largely lost touch with the ordinary working classes of Western society. And while its missionary efforts had succeeded in bringing an important ecclesial presence to every continent, the church continued to be perceived by many Asians, Africans, and Indigenous peoples of the Americas as a foreign entity—at best uninterested and dismissive, and often actively collaborating in the uncritical condemnation and suppression of their cultural and spiritual traditions.

The late Jesuit historian John O'Malley has helped us to see that over the course of the council, the bishops adopted a more open, engaging, and sympathetic approach to the

---

[6] Yves Congar, "Congar's Initial Proposals for Vatican II," Strasbourg, September 24, 1960, trans. Joseph A. Komonchak, https://jakomonchak.files.wordpress.com/2012/02/congars-plan-for-the-council.pdf.

world. Twenty-five hundred bishops from every continent gathered in this extraordinary synodal event for about three months each autumn over a four-year period. For the first time in conciliar history there was an important presence, not only of European missionary bishops, but of African and Asian Indigenous bishops who began to seize the day as agents for the renewal of the church in their own cultures and idioms. Bishops witnessed the diversity of the church and its prayer each morning as Greco-Catholic, Melkite, Maronite, Coptic, Syro-Malabar, Chaldean, and other bishops of the Eastern Catholic Churches celebrated the divine liturgy in their own liturgical traditions. Many referred to this experience as a "school for bishops." The context of the modern world in the mid-twentieth century led to a "180-degree shift in social consciousness," and with it, "a shift in how the church related to everything outside it."[7]

In both its rhetorical style and its pastoral commitments, the teaching of Vatican II elected to present the "other"—including other Christians, those of other religious traditions, nonbelievers, and indeed the whole host of peoples and cultures of humanity—in friendly terms, as bearers of truth and goodness. The council, writes O'Malley, presents "the yearning for reconciliation with the Other" as a "dominant feature" in its profile of the ideal Christian. Its "rhetoric of praise and congratulation" reflects this desire for reconciliation and collaborative engagement on multiple fronts:

> The council reconciled the relationship between bishops and pope in its instillation of collegiality in its decree on the church. The council reconciled the church with non-Western cultures in its decree on the liturgy, with other Christians in its decree on ecumen-

[7] John W. O'Malley, *When Bishops Meet: An Essay Comparing Trent, Vatican I, and Vatican II* (Cambridge, MA: Belknap Press of Harvard University Press, 2019), 193.

ism, with non-Christian religions in its decree on that subject, with non-believers in its decree on the church in the modern world, and with the modern world itself in that same decree. The council thus defined the church as essentially a reconciling institution. This was not a new idea or ideal, but the council gave it a breadth, a power, a clarity, and a dominance it had not had before.[8]

Rahner's Fundamental Theological Interpretation of the Council

Reflecting back on the experience of the council in 1979, Karl Rahner offered his "fundamental theological interpretation" of Vatican II. He was striving to understand the theological meaning and nature of these events for the nature of the church itself against the horizon of salvation history. In a profound insight that appears to be borne out with the passing of time, Rahner suggested that "the Second Vatican Council is, in a rudimentary form still groping for identity, the Church's first official self-actualization *as* a world Church."[9]

To be sure, the Christian church, as the gathering of peoples from all nations, has always been a "world church." As Lamin Sanneh has so eloquently observed, of all the great world religions, Christianity is unique in that, from the beginning, its message has been proclaimed in the idiom of diverse peoples.[10] Spreading out from Jerusalem, it set down roots in Syrian, Roman, Greek, Persian, Coptic, and Ethiopian cultures. It has never been identifiable with a single cultural

---

[8] O'Malley, *When Bishops Meet*, 30.

[9] Rahner, "Towards a Fundamental Theological Interpretation of Vatican II," 717.

[10] Lamin Sanneh, *Whose Religion Is Christianity? The Gospel beyond the West* (Grand Rapids: Wm. B. Eerdmans, 2003).

form, a single liturgical, theological, spiritual, or canonical tradition, as the council's teaching would affirm (LG 23; UR 14–17; OE 2–6). Vatican II embraced this broad perspective in its description of the church as the new people of God, "present in all the nations of the earth, and [taking] its citizens from all nations, for a kingdom which is not earthly in character but heavenly" (LG 13). The council sees the universality of the people of God in a (small "c") catholic church that "strives to recapitulate the whole of humanity and all its riches under Christ" and in the Spirit (LG 13).

Still, Rahner was obliged to admit that this identity—a realization of the church's "catholicity"—was "always a world church 'in potency,'" something less than fully realized. This was especially true in the Tridentine period when the Latin Church, now separated from the Christian East, adopted a vision of world mission identified with the project of European colonialism. "Despite the implied contradiction to its essence," he wrote, "the actual concrete activity of the Church in its relation to the world outside of Europe was in fact (if you will pardon the expression) the activity of an export firm which exported European religion as a commodity it did not really want to change but sent throughout the world together with the rest of the culture and civilization it considered superior."[11] As long as it operated within the worldview of "Christendom," the Western Church conceived of Christianity as a single, unified cultural form; too often it mistook "Romanicity" for catholicity, and uniformity for unity in faith. Rahner had no illusions about the fact that Catholicism remained highly Europeanized and Roman-centric both during and after the council. He readily admitted there is still a long and complex road to be travelled before one could speak of a church that is "inculturated throughout the world" to

[11] Rahner, "Towards a Fundamental Theological Interpretation of Vatican II," 717.

the point where one might claim it has fully actualized its identity as a world church.[12]

Still, he was able to discern in the events and teaching of Vatican II an initial realization of this new ecclesial self-consciousness. Among the signs that confirm his thesis, he pointed to the role of the college of bishops at the council as genuine protagonists, together with the bishop of Rome, in the governance of the church and in the exercise of the pastoral teaching office. He spoke of the "entire conciliar process" as a "qualitative leap" in the ways of discernment and decision-making—one that would be carried forward by the activity of the new International Synod of Bishops. He viewed the "victory of the vernacular" in the liturgy as a sure sign of the "coming to be" of a world church, one that confirms the dignity and "independence" of the local churches and calls for further inculturation. Rahner recognized in the council's teachings a shift in the church's self-awareness of its mission and agency in and for the world: "The church as a totality," he wrote, "becomes more conscious of its responsibility for the dawning history of humanity."[13] This new consciousness is expressed clearly in the Pastoral Constitution on the Church in the Modern World (*Gaudium et Spes*):

> All over the world the sense of autonomy and responsibility increases with effects of the greatest importance for the spiritual and moral maturity of humankind. This will become clearer to us if we advert to the unification of the world and the duty imposed on us to build up a better world in truth and justice. We are witnessing the birth of a new humanism, where people are defined

[12] Rahner, "Towards a Fundamental Theological Interpretation of Vatican II," 718.

[13] Rahner, "Towards a Fundamental Theological Interpretation of Vatican II," 718–19.

> before all else by their responsibility to their sisters and brothers in the court of history. (GS 55)

It was especially in its teaching on the universal salvific will of God that Rahner saw the council posing the necessary doctrinal foundations for the realization of a world church. These developments are most evident in the Declaration on the Relation of the Church to Non-Christian Religions (*Nostra Aetate*), with its positive assessment of all that is good and true in the other world religions (NA 2), and in the Declaration on Religious Liberty (*Dignitatis Humanae*). By acknowledging the dignity of every human person and the inviolable freedom of the human conscience in matters of faith, the council breaks once and for all from the triumphal model of Christendom. As Rahner put it, "The Church expressly renounces all instruments of force for the proclamation of its faith which do not lie in the power of the gospel itself."[14] Henceforth, its missional activity, following the example of Christ's own pedagogy, would rely solely on the persuasive force of an authentic witness (DH 11).

The final element of Rahner's thesis concerning the theological significance of Vatican II bears repeating here because it provides a perspective on the magnitude of this historical moment in the life of the church, a moment that he does not hesitate to describe as one of epochal change. He drew a parallel between the transition from Judaism to a "church of the Gentiles" in the first century (reflected in the account of the so-called Council of Jerusalem in the Acts of the Apostles), and from the church as a marginal group on the fringe of society to the adoption of Christianity as an official religion of the Roman Empire in the fourth century, with the end of the model of Christendom and the transition to a world church in our time. He ventured "that the differ-

---

[14] Rahner, "Towards a Fundamental Theological Interpretation of Vatican II," 720.

ence between the historical situation of Jewish Christianity and the situation into which Paul transplanted Christianity as a radically new creation is not greater than the difference between Western culture and the contemporary cultures of all Asia and Africa into which Christianity must inculturate itself if it is now to be, as it has begun to be, genuinely a world church."[15]

Can Vatican II Still Speak to the Church and World of the Twenty-First Century?

Against the horizon of this perceptive reading of Vatican II, we now turn to the question of whether Vatican II, in both its teaching and in its way of proceeding, might still have anything to say to the church and to the world in today's context, sixty years later. Let us first consider how the present context compares with that of the mid-twentieth century, as described earlier by Yves Congar.

Over the last sixty years, the human population has more than doubled and the population of Christianity has increased at a comparable pace. Today, one in three persons live either in India (now the largest country by population) or China. One in ten persons lives in extreme poverty. An unprecedented number, at last count more than one hundred million, have been displaced by violence, fear of persecution, and human rights violations. In 2021 alone, twenty-four million were forced to flee their homes due to extreme weather events and environmental devastation—floods, storms, droughts, and fires linked to the global climate crisis.[16] We are living through an unprecedented migration of peoples, one that is reshaping the ethnic and cultural mix of Christianity and urban centers everywhere.

---

[15] Rahner, "Towards a Fundamental Theological Interpretation of Vatican II," 723.

[16] UNHCR, "Global Trends Report 2021," https://www.unhcr.org/62a9d1494/global-trends-report-2021.

One out of every seven persons today claims no religious affiliation, with the unaffiliated constituting the fastest-growing religious demographic in Europe and North America. The majority of Christians now reside in the Global South. While two-thirds of the global Christian population was centered in Europe at the beginning of the twentieth century, today more than two-thirds reside in the Global South, with the largest and fastest-growing Christian presence in Africa. Demographers predict that by 2050 one in four Christians will be found in sub-Saharan Africa.[17] The world continues to struggle against the enduring consequences of colonialism, and Christians—especially in Canada, Australia, and the Amazon region—have begun to confront their complicity in the devastating effects of the history of colonization, including in the systemic suppression of the languages, cultures, and spiritual traditions of Indigenous peoples.

Finally, while women's access to education and participation in economic and political life has improved in many societies, the issues of violence against women and the prevalence of economic poverty among them are consistently identified as priorities by international human rights organizations. Similarly, while Vatican II made it possible for many women to have access to theological education and to serve in new forms of nonordained pastoral ministries, voices raised from every continent have identified the need to "rethink women's participation" in the life and ministries of the church in a way that better honors their baptismal dignity.[18]

If some of these developments were on the horizon in the

---

[17] Pew Research Center, "Global Christianity (2011)," December 19, 2011, and "The Future of World Religions: Population Growth Projections 2010–2050," April 2, 2015.

[18] General Secretariat of the Synod, "Enlarge the Space of Your Tent: Working Document for the Continental Stage," October 2022, sec. 60–70, pp. 30–34.

1960s, Vatican II had no way of predicting the dramatic rise in the human population, the emergence of a global ecological crisis accompanied by mass extinction, or a pandemic. Vatican II could not anticipate that restoring the dignity of the baptized faithful would lead to an explosion of new ecclesial ministries that still await a fuller integration into the ministerial structure of the local churches. We are living through a historic reconfiguration of ecclesial ministries (diaconal, instituted, and non-instituted lay ministries) that requires new thinking and discernment concerning the forms of ministry necessary to enable the baptized faithful to carry forward the mission of the church today. Much more remains to be done to suitably adapt the forms of liturgy, ministry, church governance, and pastoral practice so that the good news of the Gospel is no longer considered an exotic foreign reality, or the church a meeting place for those educated in Western ways. A new and effective evangelization requires a fuller inculturation of the Gospel in every context.

Carrying Forward Vatican II's Ways of Proceeding in a New Context

These are some of the important challenges facing the global Catholic Church in our time, a moment when all of humanity is confronted with grave questions concerning its very survival. If the teaching of Vatican II cannot offer a definitive answer to every question, it nonetheless offers a model for discernment and provides a theological foundation for the emergence of a world church. Pope Francis—the first bishop of Rome from the Global South—is both emblematic of that new ecclesial reality and in possession of a vision of how the orientations reflected in the experience and teaching of Vatican II continue to guide the church's way of proceeding and set us on course toward a vital realization of a world church. To conclude, I propose five points that describe essential aspects of this way of proceeding—each of them rooted in Vatican II and capable of guiding this epochal transition toward the actualization of a world church.

Trust in the Lord of History

No one expected that the elderly Pope John XXIII would call for an ecumenical council when he was elected in 1958. While on the surface the global Catholic community appeared to be just fine, he knew that beneath that institutional veneer it stood in need of deep reform, especially if it was to meet the challenges of modernity. He did not have a road map for the council or for the future direction of the human community, but called the council fathers to trust that the Lord of history would guide them as they struggled to meet the challenge of this new epoch. Rahner does not hesitate to refer to his own interpretation of these epochal transitions as a reading of "salvation history." In Jorge Bergoglio, the Catholic Church has found another pastor who invites us to trust in the presence and action of the Spirit in our time and is calling us to discern, in the signs of the times, what the Spirit is saying, aware that we stand in need of continual conversion and reform to carry out the mission of the church in our day.

The Capacity for Discerning the Gospel Has Been Entrusted to the Whole Church

Vatican II, in its recovery of the image of the church as the priestly people of God (LG 9–17) and its recognition of the dignity of the baptismal vocation, affirms the co-responsibility of all the Christian faithful for the life and mission of the church. The corollary of this insight in the council's teaching on the *sensus fidei*, the Spirit-led capacity of all the baptized to discern the truth of the Gospel (LG 12 and 35), calls for new structures of collaboration, shared discernment, and decision-making. No one person or single group of elite practitioners can claim to have sole possession of the truth, and those who exercise authority in the name of the church must call upon the gifts of all, including those with special competencies relating to the questions at hand, in arriving at their best judgment concerning the appropriate path of the community. Vatican II was itself a privileged moment in church history where the pastors of the church worked together with theologians, lay and ordained advisers, ecumenical observers, and guests to listen, learn, and discern the faith of the church. By renewing the practice of synodality, Pope Francis is calling us today to be more attentive to the sense of faith in the whole church.

The Wisdom and Diversity of the Local Churches Enriches the Catholicity of the Whole

Vatican II, like all ecumenical councils, was an expression of the shared faith and communion of all the local churches. The council's teaching on the particular churches (the term it applies to describe diocesan communities) represents a rediscovery of the dignity of the local churches in all of their diversity. As many of the bishops learned through their experience of the conciliar dialogue, the unique wisdom and experience of the churches through their insertion in diverse cultures and social contexts can be enriching for the whole church, contributing to its catholicity. Pope Francis has tried to enact this mutual enrichment in new ways—for example, through his habit of drawing from the insights of the various conferences of bishops in his teaching, or by highlighting the plight of particular communities in order to call the attention of the whole church to pressing issues. This was evident in the synod for the peoples of the Amazon region, which drew attention both to the ecological crisis and the need for a deeper inculturation of the faith that respects the cultures and tradition of Indigenous Christians.

The Conciliar Process of Vatican II Is a Step toward Recovering the Practice of Synodality

More than a perfunctory meeting of the world's Catholic bishops, Vatican II was a process that has not yet concluded. It involved a long period of consultation and preparation, with local synods meeting before and after the event. During the council sessions there were public meetings, prayers, formal and informal consultations with experts, ecumenical observers, lay and religious women and men, and commissions and subcommissions that worked both during and between each session. Since the official close of the council on December 8, 1965, we have been engaged in a protracted process of receiving the council, letting it inform and shape the life and practice of the church. The council was a synod of the global Catholic Church. Recognizing the need for a more sustained practice of synodality and collegial church governance, the council established the International Synod of Bishops, required the establishment of conferences of bishops in every country, and encouraged the establishment of other synodal bodies at diocesan and parish levels.

One of the most significant receptions of the council has been going on—often unnoticed by ordinary Catholics—in a sustained theological dialogue between the Catholic Church and other Christian churches. Vatican II's Decree on Ecumenism (*Unitatis Redintegratio*) characterized this dialogue as a humble self-examination of our own church's ways of teaching, and its forms of ecclesial life, coupled with a serious commitment to continuing renewal and reform (UR 4). As we grow together with other Christians in our understanding of the church and of the expression of its unity in structures of communion, Catholics are challenged to confront imbalances in the exercise of authority and in our practices of discernment and decision-making. Pope Francis has identified the practice of synodality—engaging all the baptized faithful in a process of mutual listening and discernment—so essential to restoring that balance in the governance of Catholic Church, as something we can learn and receive from other churches.[19] It is both a fruit of our walking together with other Christians and of great consequence for the future of Christian unity.

A World Church Is a Church in Solidarity with All of Humanity

Among the most frequently cited lines of Vatican II's teaching are the opening lines of its Pastoral Constitution on the Church in the Modern World: "The joys and hopes, the grief and anguish of the people of our time, especially of those who are poor or afflicted, are the joys and hopes, the grief and anguish of the followers of Christ as well. Nothing that is genuinely human fails to find an echo in their hearts" (GS 1). These few lines sum up the council's conviction that the place of the church is squarely *in* the world, and in solidarity with all peoples, especially with the poor and suffering. Further on, *Gaudium et Spes* spells out how the church understands its mission in this new context. Instead of bringing the good news as a "European export" to be imposed from outside (as Rahner aptly described it), the council speaks of the "law of evangelization" in terms of a shared conversation, a mutual exchange.

Next to its desire to evangelize and transform those elements of culture unaligned with the values of the Gospel, *Gaudium et Spes* acknowledges that the church itself has often been enriched as it has drawn from the wisdom and insights of various cultures, philosophies, and scientific progress. Through processes of dialogue and mutual exchange with various cultures, "new avenues to truth are opened up" and the Gospel message has been "clarified"

[19] Francis, *Evangelii Gaudium*, Apostolic Exhortation on the Joy of the Gospel (2013), sec. 246.

in the light of their wisdom (GS 44). The road to a fuller inculturation of the faith, inseparable from the work of evangelization, entails this sustained process of humble apprenticeship and Spirit-guided discernment. With faith in the Lord of history, we travel this road toward the flourishing of the world church anticipated by Vatican II.

2

A Council That Will Never End

The Unfinished Business of *Lumen Gentium*

Paul Lakeland

Let me take you back to the year of our Lord 1904, when Pope Pius X was much troubled by progressive theologians and Scripture scholars who thought that the historical background or location of texts played a part in their interpretation.[1] He called this modernism "the mother of all heresies." The year 1904 was not a good one for theologians being scrutinized and perhaps condemned by Rome, but it was a positively outstanding year for newborns destined to be great theologians, babies who would celebrate their sixtieth birthdays the year that the council fathers at the Second Vatican Council finally ratified the Dogmatic Constitution on the Church, *Lumen Gentium*. Just imagine the heartache that Cardinal Alfredo Ottaviani, the leading conservative bishop at Vatican II, president of the Holy Office and of the

[1] This chapter draws upon my previous publication, "*Lumen Gentium*: Unfinished Business," *New Blackfriars* 90, no. 1026 (2009): 146–62.

council's Doctrinal Commission, might have been saved if there had never been a Bernard Lonergan, a Karl Rahner, an Yves Congar, and a John Courtney Murray! All born that year. Lonergan's work on theological method, Rahner's attention to the horizon of mystery, Congar's elevation of the role of lay people in the church, and John Courtney Murray's vigorous defense of freedom of religion might never have happened.

Bliss would it have been for some to be alive in that particular gloom. To remain the old church would have been a veritable heaven! Transcendental Thomism would have fizzled, *la nouvelle théologie* would never have needed naming, and the council fathers would have been without a particular American Jesuit to help them come to terms with modernity. Indeed, it is possible that there might have been no council at all and the depressing letter of Pope Pius XII, *Humani Generis* (1950), might have been the last word. Or perhaps it would have been the one-session council that the curial party's damage-control apparatus fervently desired. And maybe I am overstating the importance of these four individuals, because there were others who might have carried the torch in their absence—Henri de Lubac and Jean Daniélou, Gérard Philips and Leo Joseph Suenens, among others—but one cannot deny that the face of twentieth-century Catholic theology would have been quite different without them. Suenens and Ottaviani could agree on that!

A pretentious beginning, perhaps, but one that will make clearer the reasons for the structuring of my presentation. To say that Vatican II is a council that will never end is to make a comment about the nature of tradition and the place of theological reflection in the life of the church. A couple of memorable insights from great scholars should be enough to set us on the right path. John Henry Cardinal Newman wrote the book on it, so to speak, and liked the image of a river to illustrate his understanding of tradition. Stand on the bank of a river: Is it always the same river, always the

Amazon or the Hudson? Yes, of course. But it is always moving, the water is constantly flowing, the same river is fundamentally dynamic. Perhaps the more memorable quote comes from the Yale scholar of religion Jaroslav Pelikan, who once wrote that "tradition is the living faith of the dead, traditionalism is the dead faith of the living."[2]

Back to our four 1904 newborns. In the pages that follow I consider Vatican II as a moment in this dynamic unfolding of tradition. But rather than getting bogged down in the tiresome wrangling between liberal and traditional interpretations of "the meaning of the council," I want to use the category of *renewal*. When we think about the council as an act of renewal and we wonder about unfinished business, we are asking what remains to be done to move forward the work of the council fathers. I divide these reflections into four parts, each of which focuses on one of these four babies, now grown up, who can help us along our way. Collectively, they suggest directions in which the unfinished business of Vatican II can be pursued, but not, of course, completed.

Bernard Lonergan, SJ: Historical-Mindedness and Unfinished Business

The Irish Canadian Jesuit Bernard Lonergan's fundamental insight about the work of the council is contained in his remark that "[theology] has become an empirical science in the sense that Scripture and Tradition now supply not premisses, but data."[3] What Lonergan is trying to suggest

---

[2] Jaroslav Pelikan, *The Vindication of Tradition: The 1983 Jefferson Lecture in the Humanities* (New Haven, CT: Yale University Press, 1984), 65.

[3] Bernard Lonergan, "Theology in Its New Context," in *A Second Collection*, ed. W. F. J. Ryan and B. J. Tyrell (Philadelphia: Westminster Press, 1974), 55–67, at 58.

is that the texts of the Bible and of subsequent theology are not there to be followed slavishly. They are part and parcel of the complex process of thinking through this same tradition in a changed and changing world. This helps us to make sense of the two competing theologies evident in the pages of the council documents.

Lonergan identifies the earlier form of theology as one that came into existence at the time of the Enlightenment. This "dogmatic theology" emerged in opposition to the scholastic theology that it supplanted, and "it replaced the inquiry of the *quaestio* by the pedagogy of the thesis. It demoted the quest of faith for understanding to a desirable, but secondary, and indeed, optional goal. It gave basic and central significance to the certitudes of faith, their presuppositions, and their consequences."[4]

In the twentieth century and especially at Vatican II, Lonergan thinks that a new form of theology, like the old in that it is "locked in an encounter with its age," has emerged. The new theology is empirical rather than deductive, local and particular, and evolving rather than adhering to classicist values of universality and permanence, and accompanied by a new vocabulary and imagery. The Aristotelian conceptual apparatus has gone out of fashion and very quickly "the vacuum is being refilled with biblical words and images, and with ideas worked out by historicist, personalist, phenomenological, and existential reflection."[5] Most important in what Lonergan identifies as the empirical approach is the recognition of the importance of historical context—exactly what was bothering Pius X sixty years prior. The earlier dogmatic theology talks of human nature and analyzes the human person in terms of soul and body. The new theology "adds the richer and more concrete ap-

[4] Lonergan, *A Second Collection*, 57.

[5] Lonergan, *A Second Collection*, 60.

prehension of man [*sic*] as incarnate subject."[6] It steps away from theory alone and thinks about the whole person acting in history.

What I want to suggest here is that we take Lonergan's description of the human being as incarnate subject and transfer it to the church itself. Just as when we look at the human subject in the drama of history, we find ourselves face-to-face with the question of meaning. So, when we see the church as a kind of collective incarnate subject in history, we are similarly open to the play of historical forces. In our age, says Lonergan, we have come to see that the human subject is formed by acts of meaning, that such acts proceed from free and responsible persons, that meanings differ from culture to culture and nation to nation, and that in the course of time they change, and they may go astray. Just so, the church is not a given, preserved from historical vicissitudes. Because the church is surely to be seen by Christians as vital to the implementation of God's salvific will, it does not follow that its passage through history is planned out by God, though there is divine oversight. A design is not a plan. The church is constituted anew by multiple human choices and actions, beset by national and cultural differentiation, open to change and even to decay. It is the same river, but the water is constantly moving and changing.

The unfinished business of the council to which Lonergan leads us to attend is not, then, the struggle between the classicist and the more modern approach to the meaning of church, so much as the historical conditioning of the council itself. Vatican II as an event in a story is not about the triumph, temporary or permanent, of a liberal mid-twentieth-century vision of church over the post-Tridentine, neoscholastic model. Rather, Vatican II is the demonstration

[6] Lonergan, *A Second Collection*, 61.

of the never-ending story of historical accident. The unfinished business of Vatican II to which Lonergan alerts us is that of its own contingent and nonprogrammatic character. The importance of Vatican II lies neither in the proclamation of theological novelty nor in the reiteration of timeless truths, but in its facticity as testimony to historical change. Change, remember, not progress. The unfinished business of Vatican II is a clearer understanding of how theological business is, of its nature, unfinished. What it leaves unclear is its own provisionality, and here there is something of a self-contradictory quality, for we can so easily slip into thinking of the significant reforms promoted in Vatican II as so self-evidently superior to what they replace that they can be embraced as, finally, timeless truths for our time. But the council is "locked in an encounter with its age," time-constrained and historically conditioned in its conclusions, but programmatic in its demonstration that theology is not just a product of the theological tradition, "but also of the cultural ideals and norms that set its problems and direct its solutions."[7]

Lonergan cannot, of course, leave the new theological historicism without some kind of foundation, located in a method found not in prescriptions but in "the grounds that govern the prescribing." The scientific analogy to what he is seeking in the religious realm would be something like Kuhn's scientific "paradigm shift," that fundamental change to a new model of understanding that seems to come out of nowhere, though hindsight reveals it as the mysterious result of painstaking research, and that legitimates itself in the spur it gives to further creativity. In religion, as is well known, Lonergan identifies this as the moment of "conversion." "[Conversion] is not merely a change or even a development; rather, it is a radical transformation on

[7] Lonergan, *A Second Collection*, 58.

which follows, on all levels of living, an interlocked series of changes and developments."[8]

This conversion occurs in the incarnate subject, but it can surely also be an aspect of the church as a collective incarnate subject. The council's awareness of the importance of history is nicely captured in its own phrase, "reading the signs of the times," a phrase found in the Pastoral Constitution on the Church in the Modern World, *Gaudium et Spes* (GS 4), and not in the Dogmatic Constitution on the Church, *Lumen Gentium*.[9] But there is a connection between the two: *Gaudium et Spes* enunciating the norms and strategies for engagement with the world, *Lumen Gentium* having provided the account of ecclesial conversion. Thus, a further aspect of the unfinished business of Vatican II is a new consciousness in the church of its own status as an act of ecclesial metanoia. The change of heart, however, is not to a liberal perspective rather than a conservative one; instead, it is to the historicist recognition that the meaning of the church is negotiated anew in each age, in encounter with the age. Hence the significance of the shift from the static notion of a "perfect society" to the dynamism of the historical people of God (LG 9–17). This ecclesiological insight makes attention to the age normative but does not make the insights generated in a particular age normative. What caused the demise of the classicist model was not

[8] Lonergan, *A Second Collection*, 65–66.

[9] The essay by John W. O'Malley, "Vatican II: Did Anything Happen?," in *Vatican II: Did Anything Happen?*, ed. David G. Schultenover (New York: Continuum, 2007), 52–91, brilliantly analyzes the council as an event of twentieth-century history. In the midst of continuing difference and disagreement, symbolized in the coincidence of the opening of the council and the Cuban missile crisis, *Lumen Gentium* sees the church as a sign and focus of unity. First published in *Theological Studies* 67 (2006): 3–33. See also Stephen Schloesser, "Against Forgetting: Memory, History, Vatican II," in *Vatican II: Did Anything Happen?*, 92–152.

its concrete judgments, some of which were and remain valuable, but its denial of history. In tying itself to a particular age, it tied the hands of the Gospel and denied its "productive noncontemporaneity," to use Metz's ugly but insightful phrase.[10]

Karl Rahner, SJ: The Universal Offer of God's Saving Grace

A second set of issues, located primarily in *Lumen Gentium*, hovers around the question of how Vatican II understands the relationship between the church, other Christians, and the great world religions. The puzzle, indeed, is largely of its own making, for several statements are quite hard to reconcile. There is, of course, the notoriously ambiguous claim that the one church of Christ *subsists in* the Catholic Church (see LG 8), which can be read as a generous openness to the saving significance of Christian denominations beyond the Catholic tradition, but can lead others to stress that it is the Catholic Church alone that possesses the message of salvation in its fullness. In the end, the two sides here more or less agree on the facts, but the fear factor leads them to differ on whether the ecumenical cup is half full or half empty. Of more significance might be the challenge of reconciling the bald statement that "this pilgrim church is required for salvation" (LG 14) with the evident commitment to the notion of the universal availability of salvation to be found in *Lumen Gentium*: "Nor will divine providence deny the assistance necessary for salvation to those who, without any fault of theirs, have not yet arrived at an explicit knowledge of God, and who, not without

---

[10] Johann Baptist Metz, "Productive Noncontemporaneity," in *Observations on "The Spiritual Situation of the Age": Contemporary German Perspectives*, ed. Jürgen Habermas (Cambridge, MA: MIT Press, 1985), 169–80.

grace, strive to lead a good life. Whatever of good or truth is found amongst them is considered by the church to be a preparation for the Gospel and given by him who enlightens all men and women that they may at length have life" (LG 16). While this passage continues to insist that it is through Christ that all are saved, nevertheless it imagines divine grace reaching non-Christians through their own religious traditions, and unbelievers through their human goodness.

This picture of the universal will to salvation in *Lumen Gentium* is rightly associated with the influence of Karl Rahner, but not in an uncomplicated way. For Rahner, the fact of God's universal salvific will revealed in Holy Scripture and the fact that most human beings in history have not known the Christian God leads to the inescapable conclusion that this majority are saved in Christ, but through their own traditions. While this in itself is a challenging claim on a number of fronts, it becomes the more interesting when we place it alongside Rahner's well-known utterance that in Vatican II we see "the coming of the world church."[11] The clear proclamation of a belief in the universal availability of salvation, if Rahner is correct, coincides with the end of European cultural hegemony in the Catholic Church, or at least with the beginning of the end. Rahner recognized its tentative nature and was suitably prescient about the Roman Catholic Church's efforts to stem the devolutionary tide. Nevertheless, he appears to offer a stronger reading of the words of *Lumen Gentium* cited above, when he says that they imply "the possibility of a properly salvific revelation-faith even beyond the Christian revelatory word."[12] Perhaps

---

[11] Karl Rahner, "Towards a Fundamental Theological Interpretation of Vatican II," in *Vatican II: The Unfinished Agenda*, ed. Lucien Richard, Daniel Harrington, and John W. O'Malley (New York: Paulist, 1987), 9–21, at 10.

[12] Rahner, "Towards a Fundamental Theological Interpretation of Vatican II," 14.

Rahner let his famous guard down a little here, implying that not all of God's grace must be seen as mediated through Christ. He seems to go well beyond his thesis concerning "anonymous Christians"[13] and, if he were alive and saying something like this today, might well suffer the same fate as his Jesuit brother, Roger Haight.[14]

Lumen Gentium is ambiguous about the role of the Catholic Church relative to God's will for the salvation of all. But the very ambiguity is the point. Indeed, the famously overwhelming majorities with which council documents were approved might be a sign of the council fathers recognizing the ongoing and unfinished nature of the debates, just as much if not more than the usual explanation that the documents were so equivocal that there was something for everyone to vote for. It is hard to read *Lumen Gentium* and not see a clear reiteration of the doctrine that the one church of Christ subsists in the Catholic Church. But it is also hard to read it and not see glimmers of "the possibility of a properly salvific revelation-faith even beyond the Christian revelatory word," suggested by Karl Rahner. It is also quite hard to see how the two can be smoothly reconciled.

If one of the characteristics of *Lumen Gentium* is its open-endedness on a whole variety of issues, whether we like this measure of ambiguity or not, its treatment of the universal availability of divine grace is crystal clear. The debates at the council and in subsequent decades do not put the fact into question, only the matter of its relationship to the church as the sacrament of salvation (LG 48; AG 1; GS 45). *Lumen Gentium* as an act of the council is also an act of the emergent world church. Rahner makes

---

[13] Karl Rahner, "Anonymous Christians," *Theological Investigations*, vol. 6 (New York: Crossroad, 1974), 390–98.

[14] Congregation for the Doctrine of the Faith, "Notification on the Book *Jesus Symbol of God* by Father Roger Haight, SJ," December 13, 2004.

this point very clearly, arguing that even though *Lumen Gentium* tends to be answering European problems in a European way, nevertheless it does "proclaim a universal and effective salvific will of God which is limited only by the evil decision of human conscience and nothing else," and therefore that in comparison with previous theology in general and the neoscholastic mind-set of the original council schemata, "basic presuppositions for the world mission of the world Church are fashioned which were not previously available."[15] With regard to the coming of the world church and the operations of the "universal and effective salvific will of God," the unfinished business of *Lumen Gentium* is to keep the conversation going.

Yves Congar, OP: Recovering Insights on the Laity, Bishops, and Local Church

Lumen Gentium's terminology reflects a desire to address the meaning of the church by way of *aggiornamento* and *ressourcement*. While *aggiornamento* is often translated as "bringing up to date," the connotations have more to do with a sense of renewal and refreshment rather than modernization, a term that inevitably implies the sense that we know better now. John XXIII's often-quoted remark that he wanted to open the windows and "let in a little fresh air" exactly captures the sense of *aggiornamento*. And though *ressourcement* is rightly translated as "return to the sources," we are being invited to refresh ourselves in lively springs of water gushing out of the ground, and not to bury ourselves in some moldy library basement filled with outdated answers to questions no longer asked. *Ressourcement*, for the most part, means to revisit the inspiration of the great fathers and mothers of the church, each of them

[15] Rahner, "Towards a Fundamental Theological Interpretation of Vatican II," 14.

distinguished by their clear commitment to an encounter with their own age, whether it be an Origen or an Augustine or an Aquinas. In each and every case, *ressourcement* means reading them in their own historical context, not as some stultifying system. They are, in Lonergan's felicitous phrase, "not premisses, but data."

There was no better twentieth-century exponent of the balance between *aggiornamento* and *ressourcement* than Yves Congar, who championed the movement of *la nouvelle théologie*, devoted as it was to the rehistoricizing of Christian tradition in the face of neoscholasticism and the aftermath of the modernist crisis. It was, indeed, the prominent neoscholastic Dominican theologian Reginald Garrigou-Lagrange who sarcastically labeled Congar, Marie-Dominique Chenu, and others as the "new theologians" and who aided Pius XII's attack on them in his 1950 encyclical, *Humani Generis*. His hatred for them, not too strong a word, was due as much to the plan of study of the Dominican seminary Le Saulchoir, outlined by Chenu in a privately circulated manuscript in the late 1930s,[16] a text that led to his eventual removal from the seminary and long-term exile to Canada,[17] as it was to any work by

[16] It was Chenu in this text who really developed the idea of the importance of "reading the signs of the times," and it was Chenu who had the greatest influence on the text of *Gaudium et Spes*. Both Joseph Ratzinger and Karl Rahner declared that the text was too optimistic and that it underplayed "the cross" in favor of "the incarnation." See Marie-Dominique Chenu, *Une école de théologie: Le Saulchoir* (privately printed at Le Saulchoir, 1937; reprinted as *Une école de théologie: Le Saulchoir avec les études de Giuseppe Alberigo, Étienne Fouilloux, Jean Ladrière et Jean-Pierre Jossua* [Paris: Les Éditions du Cerf, 1985], 95–173); see also Étienne Fouilloux, "L'affaire Chenu: 1937–1943," *Revue des sciences philosophiques et théologiques* 98 (2014): 261–352, at 267 and 287–288.

[17] There is an amusing essay to be written on the various places of exile to which suspect French theologians were sent in the 1950s. Not for them any Devil's Island, unless the theological equivalent

Congar, Jean Daniélou, or Henri de Lubac, the other primary objects of his wrath. Chenu's schematic outline of the course of study at Le Saulchoir stressed reading tradition in a historically sensitive manner, an approach that raised once more the shibboleths of the modernist witch hunt.

While Chenu had the greater influence on *Gaudium et Spes*, it was Congar whose thought ran through and through the text of *Lumen Gentium*. The stress on the central significance of the baptismal priesthood, the prominence of the role of the laity, the historical recall of episcopal collegiality, the location of ecclesiastical authority in the work of the Holy Spirit—all can be traced to Congar's ideas in his great work of the early fifties, *Jalons pour une théologie du laïcat* (*Lay People in the Church*).[18] He was by no means the only one—Gérard Philips was another[19]—but Congar's was the single biggest influence. However, and somewhat ironically, the completion of *Lumen Gentium* coincided almost exactly with a radical revision in Congar's own ecclesiology.

While *Lumen Gentium* has several areas of unfinished business, some of the more important of which we have touched on in this paper, the way in which Congar addressed his own and *Lumen Gentium*'s treatment of the laity as "secular" is instructive for the way in which unfinished business needs to be conducted. In the original edition of *Lay People in the Church*, Congar had written of the laity as those who do God's work in the world, those for whom

---

of such might be Canada (Chenu), Cambridge, England, and later Jerusalem (Congar), or, most improbable of all for a Frenchman, Daniélou's internal exile from the Jesuit house of studies at Fourvière near Lyons to Paris (!), where he became chaplain to a girls' *lycée*.

[18] Yves Congar, *Jalons pour une théologie du laïcat* (Paris: Cerf, 1953). English translation: *Lay People in the Church: A Study for a Theology of Laity*, trans. Donald Attwater (London: Geoffrey Chapman, 1959).

[19] Gérard Philips, *The Role of the Laity in the Church*, trans. John R. Gilbert and James W. Moudry (Chicago: Fides, 1956).

"the substance of things in themselves is real and interesting," while the cleric is the one "for whom things are not really interesting *in themselves*, but for something other than themselves, namely, their relation to God."[20] In *Lumen Gentium* this becomes a reference to the "secular character" that is "proper and peculiar" to the laity, for "it is the special vocation of the laity to seek the kingdom of God by engaging in temporal affairs and directing them according to God's will" (LG 31). By this time Congar was revising his work to take account of criticism that he failed to break away from the clergy/laity division, and increasingly he began to write about "different ministries" rather than different classes of people. By the end of his life, he could comment on the earlier Congar as someone who had fallen into the trap of defining the laity relative to the clergy and go on to make the quite different claim that "today it is the case, rather, that the clergy need to be defined in relation to the laity, who are quite simply members of the people of God animated by the Spirit."[21]

Congar's work deeply influenced Vatican II's teaching on the office of bishop in service to the local church and its communion with the other local churches, a bond that finds expression in the collegial nature of the episcopate. If we were to try to draw up a list of those teachings of Vatican II that seem in the intervening years to have been more honored in the breach than in the observance, that of the collegiality of the bishops would be very high on the list. From the notorious *nota praevia explicativa* (preliminary explanatory note) attached to the text of *Lumen Gentium* at the express order of the pope,[22] whether Paul VI intended

[20] Congar, *Lay People in the Church*, 17.

[21] The comments are recorded in *Fifty Years of Catholic Theology: Conversations with Yves Congar*, ed. and introduced by Bernard Lauret, trans. John Bowden (Philadelphia: Fortress, 1988), 65–66.

[22] John O'Malley, *What Happened at Vatican II?* (Cambridge, MA:

to protect an overwhelming "yes" vote or to undercut the council's teachings, to the evisceration of the International Synod of Bishops that Paul had at first seemed to favor, to John Paul II's clever but destructive distinction between "affective" and "effective" collegiality,[23] all have conspired to subvert *Lumen Gentium*'s evident intention to put the bugbear of conciliarism to rest. *Lumen Gentium* attempted to finesse the delicate balance of papal and conciliar authority by expressing them as two manifestations of the guidance of the Holy Spirit. Together with the third way the Spirit guides the church, the so-called *sensus fidei* (the sense of faith among all the baptized; cf. LG 12), these three cannot legitimately be in competition with one another, for the Spirit cannot be at war with itself. Nor, as befits a Trinitarian analogue, is there any priority among the three, though difference is surely present. We might say they have different roles in the economy of the church, but *in esse* they are nothing more than the one power of the Holy Spirit, watching over God's church.

As time has elapsed since the council's work, it has become more and more apparent that the discussion of collegiality is an instance of a more fundamental concern, that of the balance between the local and the universal church. One would have thought that the council fathers' resounding opinion that a bishop becomes bishop in virtue of his ordination (LG 21) and not by some papal act of delegation (LG 27) would have set this issue to rest, not to mention *Lumen Gentium*'s firm insistence that the local church possesses all the elements of the whole church and is not a branch office of some ecclesiastical transnational (SC

Belknap Press of Harvard University Press, 2008), 238–45, at 244–45.

[23] For a discussion of this tactic, see Lakeland, "John Paul II and Collegiality," in *The Vision of John Paul II: Assessing His Thought and Influence*, ed. Gerard Mannion (Collegeville, MN: Liturgical Press, 2008), 184–99, at 192–94.

41; LG 23). That this is not the case was apparent in the extraordinarily frank exchanges at the turn of the century between Cardinal Walter Kasper, champion of the priority of the local church, and Cardinal Josef Ratzinger, patron of the priority of the universal church.[24] The open-ended nature of this particular debate, though it ceased when Cardinal Ratzinger became pope in 2005, is in itself a part of the ongoing unfinished business of *Lumen Gentium*. Extreme conciliarism (the theory that church councils can overrule and depose the pope) and extreme papalism (which conceives of the pope as an absolute monarch) both attempt to foreclose debate and fail to recognize the delicate balance that *Lumen Gentium* sought to express. Indeed, the decline of the fortunes of collegiality and of the legitimate autonomy of the local church in the last two or three decades is a product of efforts to frustrate the intentions of *Lumen Gentium*. *Lumen Gentium* did not seek, let us be clear, to overturn the papalism of Vatican I in favor of a return to the Council of Constance, but tried very hard to put both pope and council in a pneumatological context. The unfinished business of *Lumen Gentium* is to strive to keep the delicate balance alive.

The then-cardinal Ratzinger was right to insist that the universal church is not simply a federation of local churches.

---

[24] Kasper takes on Ratzinger initially in a book chapter, "Zur Theologie und Praxis des bischöflichen Amtes," in *Auf neue Art Kirche Sein: Wirklichkeiten—Herausforderungen—Wandlungen* (Munich: Bernward bei Don Bosco, 1999), 32–48. Ratzinger responded in an article in the *Frankfurter Allgemeine Zeitung* (December 22, 2000), 46. Kasper argued further in "On the Church: A Friendly Response to Cardinal Ratzinger," *America* 184 (April 21–30, 2001), and was answered yet again by Cardinal Ratzinger in "A Response to Walter Kasper: The Local Church and the Universal Church," *America* 185 (November 19, 2001). The easiest approach to this complicated set of exchanges is provided by an excellent overview from Kilian McDonnell, "The Ratzinger/Kasper Debate: The Universal Church and Local Churches," *Theological Studies* 63 (2002): 227–50.

Lumen Gentium said as much. But Cardinal Kasper was equally correct to point out that there is no universal church aside from or prior to the local churches of which it is composed. What neither of them seems to have considered, but which may be important to our consideration of unfinished business, is the extent to which local churches—reflecting their cultures—might take on somewhat different external forms from one another.

John Courtney Murray, SJ: Freedom of Religion—Receiving the Insight of a Local Church

Whether one is committed to the priority of the universal over the local church or the opposite, one can still value the special contributions of local churches, destined to become increasingly apparent to the degree that the Catholic Church is becoming more and more a world church. Ironically enough, at Vatican II the local church whose culture had the most impact upon the council documents was the American Catholic Church, which is certainly not what comes to mind when we think of an emerging world church. Yet it is hard not to see the significance of the American democratic experiment in the council's Declaration on Religious Liberty (*Dignitatis Humanae*), and not easy to overestimate the contribution of the American Jesuit John Courtney Murray to the sea change that came about in the Catholic Church's understanding of its place in democratic societies. When we explore in more detail, we discover that the insights of American democratic life return us to deep-seated Catholic roots. And nothing could provide us with a better example of the symbiotic relationship between the local and the universal church proclaimed in *Lumen Gentium* than Vatican II's treatment of freedom of religion.

The genius of John Courtney Murray's influence on *Dignitatis Humanae* is the way in which the document reflects the wisdom of American experience with religion and democracy, while formulating its discussion of religious freedom in terms not of rights or conscience but rather as an application of natural law. Nineteenth-century continental European suspicion of the so-called Americanist heresy was fueled by the assumption that the disestablishment of religion meant its restriction by and subordination to the power of the state. In the United States, however, separation of powers was a mechanism developed to provide for the free exercise of religion and to keep religion in general and that of the majority in particular from undue influence in secular government. But Murray's influence on the council fathers leads them beyond this kind of pragmatic argument to one in which the divine law requires individuals to seek truth, especially religious truth. This search "must be carried out in a manner that is appropriate to the dignity . . . of the human person: that is, by free enquiry" (DH 3).

It is a curiosity to which not enough attention has been devoted (Joseph Komonchak is an honorable exception here[25]) that Vatican II in general and *Lumen Gentium* in particular represent not so much a struggle between a premodern and a modern church as one between two distinguishable strands of modernism. In *Lumen Gentium*'s openness to the future and in *Dignitatis Humanae*'s forceful advocacy for freedom of conscience in religion we can see Enlightenment values at work, values that—as the Canadian philosopher Charles Taylor has pointed out—are values the church needed to learn from modernity itself.[26]

In the resistance to these conciliar priorities we encounter another modernity, described by Komonchak as the effort to harness elements of modernity to create a "counter-modern

---

[25] See Joseph A. Komonchak, "Modernity and the Construction of Roman Catholicism," *Cristianesimo nella storia* 18 (1997): 353–85.

[26] Charles Taylor, "A Catholic Modernity?," in *A Catholic Modernity?: Charles Taylor's Marianist Award Lecture*, ed. James L. Heft (New York: Oxford University Press, 1999), 13–37, especially 16–18.

church" whose authority "represents a classic illustration of that self-conscious, rationalized, and bureaucratized mode of thought in which Max Weber saw the distinctive mark of modernity."[27] Taylor, on his part, puts the resistance to the openness toward modernity down not to Christianity itself, but to "the project of Christendom: the attempt to marry the faith with a form of culture and a mode of society."[28] So, more important than the details of *Dignitatis Humanae* is the relationship established between the teaching of the universal church and the culturally conditioned contribution of any local church, in this case that of the United States of America. Attention to the local church as a culturally distinct contributor to the reality of the universal church is a defense against Christendom and a challenge to bureaucratized thinking.

Once again, we see that the unfinished business of *Lumen Gentium* is not to decide for the local church against the universal church, but to maintain the two in right relationship to and in delicate balance with one another. The effort to foreclose the open-ended debate does not come from those who want to give some priority to the universal church, or at least not because they want to give such priority, but from those who cannot see the futility of the Christendom project. We should also remember that modernity itself, which so colors the liberal "wing" of the council fathers, is not far from Christendom in its unthinkingly hegemonic assumptions about the perspectives of Western culture. Here, where modernity shades into postmodernity and the local and particular have voice over the universal, beyond metanarratives about the triumph of the West, of Christendom or of the church, may be where we find the free space in which to continue the unfinished business of

[27] Komonchak, "Modernity and the Construction of Roman Catholicism," 383.

[28] Taylor, "A Catholic Modernity?," 17.

walking the tightrope between anarchic particularism and authoritarian universalism. We should not have to choose between the good of the part and the good of the whole.

A Dance to the Music of Time

Anthony Powell's English response to Proust, *A Dance to the Music of Time*, displays the historical realism of narrative without closure.[29] In its unwillingness to tell a story equipped with a beginning, middle, and end, the theology of *Lumen Gentium* is much more like this than we might imagine. Like Powell's great work, an awful lot is happening of great interest and relevance to the moment, but it is not rushing toward some denouement, perhaps not even going anywhere in particular. It is the journey, not the arrival; that is the point. As Komonchak has suggested, on the inside of history we can tell about as many stories as there are starting points to choose from. From a point within the pattern, the overall design cannot itself be determined. For someone like Powell, there is no design, but all is chance. For a theist there must be a design if not a story, but even for the theist it cannot be discerned from within. Only from a God's-eye view is it visible. For this reason, if for no other, the faith of the believer, the faith of the church, is not so much faith in a particular discernible end to history, but rather fidelity to hope in God's saving design for us. Eschatological hope is not utopian longing.

To think of Vatican II as an event in a series bounded by an eschatological horizon allows for the emergence of the genuinely novel without the expectation of progress toward an intrahistorical terminus. The reign of God is all around us, within history, or constantly breaking into history, but not exactly being constructed as a historical phenomenon.

[29] Anthony Powell, *A Dance to the Music of Time*, 12 vols. (London: Heinemann, 1951–1975).

The church, as both proleptic of the reign of God and a sacrament of the reign of God, can engage in reform or revolution, and perhaps should do so from time to time, though not in order to make more progress. Change in the church is renewal or, perhaps better, refreshment. Refreshment takes place, in Lonergan's terms, when the church is "locked in an encounter with its age," reading the signs of the times and striving to be for its own time that community within which the transcendent is celebrated and hoped for, in an eschatological rather than a historical horizon. Both *Lumen Gentium* and *Gaudium et Spes* see the church in this way. We are a pilgrim people, says *Lumen Gentium*, but the pilgrimage we are on is directed to the reign of God, not to a historical utopia.

We travel in hope and if we lose our way for a time, it will not be because the map went missing, but because we forgot the kind of journey we were on. Perhaps we thought there was just one way to go, or some kind of shortcut to get "there," wherever "there" is. Christendom, neo-scholasticism, a centralizing papacy, these are all so many misdirections for the pilgrim people not because they are conservative or "on the right" on some ideological spectrum, but because they have forgotten that eschatological hope, while it is within history, is not hope in any historical fix. The healthiest moments in church history have been those where divine providence has not been mistaken for historical progress, indeed where we as a people have not been so sure where exactly we are "going," if we are "going" anywhere at all. To a degree, our postmodern world with its suspicion of universal reason and controlling metanarratives offers the church a way beyond the instrumental rationality of modernity with which it has been infected. And when we look back with apparent nostalgia to the early church, the church of the first three centuries, it should not be because we think they had everything right or they were more liberal than we are or more conservative than we are. A historical judgment would suggest that they had many challenges to their own self-understanding and almost literally did not know where they were going. But theirs was a far more pluralistic age than ours, which means one in which everything except eschatological hope in the reign of the kingdom is in question. It is in this sense, quite unromantic, that the early age might be a model for us now.

The example of an architect of *Lumen Gentium* having second and third thoughts about his own earlier ideas, ideas that influenced the text of the council document, brings us to a final dimension of the unfinished business, which is not to canonize the particular insights of *Lumen Gentium*. If *aggiornamento/ressourcement* is the theological method of refreshing the church, it is the method rather than this or that particular judgment that needs to be the focus of unfinished business. Times change, and if theology is "locked in an encounter with its age," then theological insights that were important at one time may take a back seat at another.[30] Once again, looking at things this way puts the typical representation of the postconciliar era as a standoff between liberals and conservatives into question. While conservatives are undoubtedly at fault if they tie themselves to a historically conditioned theological system as if it were exempt from historicity, liberals can similarly be endangered by clinging to the insights of *Lumen Gentium* as if it were about to become the new dogmatics. *Lumen Gentium* is not "the truth." It is an effort to refresh the horizon of eschatological hope for a particular age. Sixty years on, its ideas have not been fully implemented in part because of ecclesiastical intransigence, in part because sixty years means that some of the ideas are already dated. Times

---

[30] On the volatility of theological truths, there is no better analysis than that to be found in John E. Thiel, *Senses of Tradition: Continuity and Development in Catholic Faith* (New York: Oxford University Press, 2000).

change, and the final unfinished business of *Lumen Gentium* may be to declare it both a historical document whose time is beginning to be past, and a glorious effort to demonstrate the restoration of historical awareness in official theology. *Lumen Gentium* is "not premisses but data."

3

Reform in Motion

Vatican II and the Liturgy

John F. Baldovin, SJ

Twenty years ago I was having a conversation with the Belgian liturgical scholar Paul DeClerck. We were talking about the state of Catholic liturgy in North America and Northern Europe in particular. One thing he said stayed with me: "How is it that after forty years we have still not succeeded in helping people to understand that the liturgy is a truly communal event?" I'm afraid that we still have a long way to go twenty years later as we celebrate the sixtieth anniversary of the opening of the Second Vatican Council. And so, our title: "Reform in Motion."

I have two premises for this essay. The first is that the Constitution on the Sacred Liturgy (*Sacrosanctum Concilium*) and the subsequent implementation of the reform need to be understood in the framework of a comprehensive renewal in ecclesiology, a renewed vision of the church. The second is that the reform has yet to be digested or assimilated by many if not the majority of Catholics.

I am going to proceed in three parts and a final conclusion. In the first part I deal with the theological and ecclesiological vision that undergirds the Constitution on the Sacred Liturgy and how that vision relates to the other three constitutions of Vatican II. In the second I discuss how the specific reforms that *Sacrosanctum Concilium* mandated are intended to make that vision a reality. My third part deals with the reception of the reformed liturgies and especially with Pope Francis's reaffirmation of the liturgical reform. I conclude with some suggestions for a way forward.

Liturgy in the Context of a Renewed Liturgical Theology and Ecclesiology

Let me start here with two fundamental paragraphs of *Sacrosanctum Concilium*. The first is *Sacrosanctum Concilium* 7:

> To accomplish so great a work [the celebration of the paschal mystery], Christ is always present in his church, especially in liturgical celebrations. He is present in the sacrifice of the Mass, both in the person of his minister, "the same now offering, through the ministry of priests, who formerly offered himself on the cross," and most of all in the eucharistic species. By his power he is present in the sacraments, so that when anybody baptizes it is really Christ himself who baptizes. He is present in his word, since it is he himself who speaks when the holy scriptures are read in church. Lastly, he is present when the church prays and sings, for he has promised: "where two or three are gathered together in my name, there am I in the midst of them" (Mt 18:20).
>
> Christ, indeed, always associates the church with himself in this great work in which God is perfectly glorified and men and women are sanctified. The church is his beloved bride who calls to its Lord, and through him offers worship to the eternal Father.

> The liturgy, then, is rightly seen as an exercise of the priestly office of Jesus Christ. . . .
>
> From this it follows that every liturgical celebration, because it is an action of Christ the priest and of his body, which is the church, is a preeminently sacred action. No other action of the church equals its effectiveness by the same title nor to the same degree.

Please note that it is *Christ* here who is the primary actor in the liturgy. The Catholic conviction is that Christ is present and active here and now—*and* that he acts in concert with the assembled church community. As the Eucharistic Prayer for Use in Masses for Various Needs I puts it so beautifully after the *Holy, Holy, Holy* acclamation:

> Blessed indeed is your Son,
> present in our midst
> when we are gathered by his love
> and when, as once for the disciples, *so now for us,*
> he opens the Scriptures and breaks the bread.

The present action of Christ in the liturgy is also wonderfully expressed in the Prayer over the Offerings for Holy Thursday (which is repeated on the Second Sunday of Ordinary Time):

> Grant us, O Lord, we pray,
> that we may participate worthily in these mysteries,
> for whenever the memorial of this sacrifice
> is celebrated
> *the work of our redemption is accomplished.*

To put it simply—all that Christ is and what Christ has done for us by bringing us into communion with God is present every time we celebrate the liturgy. I want to emphasize the "*we celebrate.*" *Sacrosanctum Concilium* 7 makes it quite clear that Christ is acting within the body that is the church—head and members. Let me emphasize that this is an essential ecclesiological move in the whole council—a point that is repeated in *Sacrosanctum Concilium* 26 and 27 as well:

> Liturgical services are not private functions, but are celebrations of the church, which is the "sacrament of unity," namely, the holy people united and organized under their bishops.
>
> Therefore, liturgical services have to do with the whole body, the church. They make it visible and have effects upon it. But they also touch individual members of the church in different ways, depending on their ranks, roles and levels of participation. (SC 26)

> It must be emphasized that rites which are meant to be celebrated in common, with the faithful present and actively participating, should as far as possible be celebrated in that way rather than by an individual and quasi-privately. (SC 27)

This is not a theme that is confined to the Constitution on the Sacred Liturgy. It forms one of the most significant guiding principles of the Dogmatic Constitution on the Church (*Lumen Gentium*), especially in *Lumen Gentium* 9–17 on "the People of God." *Lumen Gentium* 10–11 underlines the sacramental nature of the church, the church understood not primarily as an institution but rather as the baptized priestly people of God:

> Christ the Lord, high priest taken from the midst of humanity (see Heb 5:1–5), made the new people "a kingdom of priests to his God and Father" (Apoc 1:6; see 5:9–10). The baptized, by regeneration and

> the anointing of the holy Spirit, are consecrated as a spiritual house and a holy priesthood, that through all their Christian activities they may offer spiritual sacrifices and proclaim the marvels of him who has called them out of darkness into his wonderful light (see 1 Pet 2:4–10). Therefore, all the disciples of Christ, persevering in prayer and praising God (see Acts 2:42–47), should present themselves as a sacrifice, living, holy, and pleasing to God (see Rom 12:1). They should everywhere on earth bear witness to Christ and give an answer to everyone who asks a reason for their hope of eternal life (see 1 Pet 3:15). (LG 10)
>
> . . . Taking part in the Eucharistic sacrifice, the source and summit of the Christian life, *they offer the divine victim to God and themselves along with him.* (LG 11)

Here is one example of why the council with its sixteen documents must be understood as a whole, as the historian Massimo Faggioli as well as others have repeatedly argued.[1]

Allow me to illustrate this further with a second crucial paragraph of *Sacrosanctum Concilium*, perhaps the best known and most quoted—14:

> It is very much the wish of the church that all the faithful should be led to take that full, conscious, and active part in liturgical celebrations which is demanded by the very nature of the liturgy, and to which the Christian people, "a chosen race, a royal priesthood, a holy nation, a redeemed people" (1 Pet 2:9, 4–5) have a right and to which they are bound by reason of their Baptism.

---

[1] Massimo Faggioli, *Vatican II: The Battle for Meaning* (Mahwah, NJ: Paulist Press, 2012), 125–33.

Notice: the "very nature of the liturgy" demands full conscious and active participation—a participation that builds upon but goes further than the interiorization of the liturgy implied by the paragraphs I cited earlier with regard to the presence of Christ in his Body, the church. This participation is our right, *our right*, by reason of our baptism. When you think about it—this is a remarkable statement that has all sorts of implications about how we relate to one another in the liturgy, far transcending the distinctions between lay and clergy. The council does not use the phrase "baptismal ecclesiology," but that is precisely what is being affirmed in this paragraph as well as *Sacrosanctum Concilium* 7, which I cited earlier. In the mind of the council, the reformed Catholic liturgy is not a spectator sport but a team sport, involving a number of ministers enacting important roles and serving the entire assembly's participation.

In addition, this baptismal ecclesiology provides solid grounding for understanding the ecumenical significance of the council. What binds baptized Christians together is far more important than what divides us. The ecumenical importance of the liturgical reform is noted in the very first paragraph of *Sacrosanctum Concilium*: "to encourage whatever can promote the union of all who believe in Christ" (SC 1). In what has been referred to as the current "ecumenical winter" in the church we need to realize that we have a long way to go with regard to ecumenism.

Let me sum up: *Sacrosanctum Concilium* is solidly grounded in the conviction that Christ is the primary actor in the liturgy, Christ acting in the Body which is the church. And Christ acting in the Body of Christ is further grounded in what I am calling baptismal ecclesiology. This means that the primary manifestation of the church, not the only but the primary, takes place when the church, the particular assembly of the faithful, gathers to worship God as paragraph 2 of *Sacrosanctum Concilium* affirms.

Before I turn to my second part—the specific reforms and their implementation in the wake of the council—I need to make good on my promise to relate *Sacrosanctum Concilium* to the other two major constitutions of Vatican II—namely the Dogmatic Constitution on Divine Revelation (*Dei Verbum*) and the Pastoral Constitution on the Church in the Modern World (*Gaudium et Spes*).

As is frequently noted, the liturgical movement, the biblical movement, and the ecumenical movement all go hand in hand. Each resulted in one way or another from a dissatisfaction with the rigid Catholic theology that became common after the Council of Trent in the sixteenth century, often referred to as neoscholasticism. By the mid-nineteenth century the time was ripe for a new way of doing theology, a way that in reality relied heavily on an *older* way of doing theology—a return to the sources, usually known by its French name, *ressourcement*. At the same time, Protestant theologians and biblical scholars were becoming more and more aware of the need to study texts and to do history in a more critical fashion.[2]

Two results of the coincidence of the biblical and liturgical revivals were: first, the realization of just how thoroughly biblical the liturgy is (e.g., the chants, the readings, and the inspiration of its prayers), and second, that the eucharistic liturgy needed to incorporate far more of the scriptural texts than had been the case since the early Middle Ages where the Sunday texts were limited to a one-year cycle with two readings for each Sunday and feast and rarely a reading from the Old Testament. This is reflected in *Sacrosanctum Concilium* 24: "Sacred Scripture is of the greatest importance in the celebration of the liturgy. For from it are drawn

[2] For further detail, see John F. Baldovin, "The Development of the Liturgy: Theological and Historical Roots of *Sacrosanctum Concilium*," *Worship* 87, no. 6 (November 2013): 517–32.

the lessons which are read and which are explained in the homily; from it too come the psalms which are sung. It is from Scripture that the petitions, prayers and hymns draw their inspiration and their force, and that actions and signs derive their meaning."

The last sentence here is crucial. To put it bluntly: no Scripture, no liturgy. The importance of the Scriptures is reiterated in *Sacrosanctum Concilium* 51 with regard to the Eucharist: "The treasures of the Bible are to be opened up more lavishly, so that a *richer fare* may be provided for the faithful at the table of God's word. In this way the more significant part of the Sacred Scriptures will be read to the people over a fixed number of years."

The result, as you know, was a three-year lectionary cycle for Sundays and major feasts, a cycle that includes ample selections from the Old Testament and covers each of the four Gospels, since each Sunday and solemnity has three readings: one from the Old Testament, another from a non-Gospel New Testament book, and the third from the Gospels. The exception is the Easter season, where the first reading is taken from the Acts of the Apostles according to tradition. The revised lectionary also contained a two-year weekday cycle that was based on a continuous reading of Scripture from both the Old and the New Testaments. Moreover, for the first time in the history of the church, proper readings were provided for every day of the year. (Hitherto daily readings were provided only for the weekdays of Lent.) The conclusion is that renewed Catholic appreciation of the Bible and the place of the Bible in the Constitution on the Sacred Liturgy go hand in hand.

Moreover, chapter 6 of the Dogmatic Constitution on Divine Revelation ("Sacred Scripture in the Life of the Church") explicitly refers to the place of Scripture in the liturgy (DV 21). I would add that a number of scholars, including the Lutheran Gordon Lathrop and the Catholics Louis-Marie Chauvet and Goffredo Boselli, have argued that the liturgy itself as proclaimed in the midst of the church assembled for worship is the native home of Scripture—both in terms of the birth of the Bible itself and in terms of its living interpretation today.[3]

I have yet to say anything about the relation between *Sacrosanctum Concilium* and the final great constitution of the council—the Pastoral Constitution on the Church in the Modern World (*Gaudium et Spes*). There, although *Sacrosanctum Concilium* is not explicitly mentioned, *Gaudium et Spes* situates human activity firmly within the context of the food for the journey that the Lord has provided for us in the Eucharist (GS 38).

All the foregoing is, in a sense, a prelude to the second part.

How Did the Implementation of the Reforms Realize the Vision of Sacrosanctum Concilium?

The reform of the liturgy as envisioned by the Constitution on the Sacred Liturgy of 1963 was embodied and brought to fruition by an entire library of books of the revised Roman Rite. In fact, over time many of them have been published in second or even third editions. And as we in the English-speaking world are all too well aware, our translations have been revised as well.

We should note the speed with which Pope Paul VI's commission to implement *Sacrosanctum Concilium* did its work. The work, which began under the direction of Father

[3] Gordon Lathrop, *The Four Gospels on Sunday: The New Testament and the Reform of Christian Worship* (Minneapolis: Fortress, 2012), 153–55; Louis-Marie Chauvet, *Symbol and Sacrament: A Sacramental Reinterpretation of Christian Existence*, trans. Barry Hudock (Collegeville, MN: Liturgical Press, 1995), 190–227; Goffredo Boselli, *The Spiritual Meaning of the Liturgy: School of Prayer, Source of Life* (Collegeville, MN: Liturgical Press, 2014), 47–78, 112–18.

(later Archbishop) Annibale Bugnini in 1964, was by and large finished by 1972.[4] This was a remarkable achievement in just eight years. The commission (or *Consilium* as it was named), consisting mainly of experts in the various subfields of liturgy, produced the texts in Latin. It was left to the various national bishops' conferences to produce translations of the texts. Even during the council, bishops from the various language groups (mainly French, German, and English) realized that many individual bishops' conferences did not have the resources to produce the translated books of the reformed Roman Rite and so was born the English Commission for the Translation of the Liturgy (usually abbreviated as ICEL). ICEL, consisting of eleven bishops representing their own and also nineteen smaller associated conferences, was aided by a secretariat that organized a large number of experts in linguistics, Scripture, history, pastoral reflection, and theology to do the challenging work of translation.

What was accomplished? I mention here nine features of the liturgy that were significantly affected by the reform. Keep in mind that the basic motivation for all of this change was a renewed understanding of how Christ acts in the liturgy in concert with the whole of the common priesthood, a baptismal ecclesiological vision.

The first and probably the most significant feature was the project of translation itself. Even before the council ended it was obvious to many bishops representing different nations that for the liturgical vision to be implemented, the whole of the liturgy needed to be translated into the language of the people, the vernacular. In 1969 a strategy of transla-

[4] It could be argued that the reform actually began with the liturgical commission established by Pope Pius XII in 1948 following his landmark encyclical on the liturgy, *Mediator Dei* (1947). See Annibale Bugnini, *The Reform of the Liturgy, 1948–1975*, trans. Matthew J. O'Connell (Collegeville, MN: Liturgical Press, 1990), 6–13. Bugnini was the secretary to the first commission.

tion was provided by the document that came out of the Congregation for Divine Worship titled *Comme le prévoit*. (Notice: the original was written in French, not the usual Latin of official documents.) *Comme le prévoit* adopted a modern theory of translation called dynamic equivalence, a theory that puts an emphasis on making the original texts intelligible in the various languages. This theory and its application were originally devised by Dr. Eugene Nida, who himself was responsible for the Bible translation that is now called *The Good News Bible: Today's English Version*.

The second feature, and no less important, was the vastly expanded repertoire of Scripture passages that has expanded an ever-increasing biblical literacy and scriptural spirituality among Catholics. I should acknowledge that much more work needs to be done in this regard—both in preaching and catechesis.

From this point on, these reforms aren't ranked, but I simply list them without ranking one as more important than another.

A third feature of the revised books was the addition of a robust introduction (referred to as *Praenotanda*) for each of the rites. For the first time in the history of the church (at least as far as I can tell), an introduction to each rite contained more than just laws, rules, and rubrics. Rather, these rules were contextualized by a theology without which they are not very compelling. In my opinion, people who deal pastorally with the liturgy do not pay enough attention to these introductions. Often enough we look at them for answers to specific questions (what color vestment should be worn for a wedding?) rather than for the inspiration of a theological/spiritual vision.

Next, in accord with *Sacrosanctum Concilium* 21, 23, 27, and especially 34, the liturgical rites themselves were greatly simplified, and accretions over time, like barnacles on a ship, were stripped away to enable the genius of the rite to be revealed. A good example is the revision of the old Offertory Rite in the Mass, which contained numerous prayers said inaudibly by the priest. It constituted a virtual replication of the Roman Canon or Eucharistic Prayer. This rite was revised as the Presentation of the Gifts and the Preparation of the Altar—a revision that now clearly features the participation of the people in presenting the offerings.

My fifth feature is the revision of the various sacramental rites. Prominent among these revisions was the provision of a rite specifically geared to the baptism of children (for the first time in the church's history!), a restored catechumenate (RCIA), a revision of the rites of penance to provide for more communal celebration in line with *Sacrosanctum Concilium* 26 and 27, and a rite for the anointing of the sick that is inspired by a model of pastoral care, and moves from the older notion of a deathbed ritual (extreme unction) to a prayer for spiritual and physical healing in light of serious illness.

Further, in tune with the desire to promote more full, conscious, and active participation in the liturgy, the commission mandated that the main altar in each church should be free-standing, that is, separated from the back wall, so that the Eucharist could be celebrated facing the people (*versus populum*).

The Liturgy of the Hours was radically revised with the intent that it become the daily prayer of the people of God. The Psalter was now spread out over four weeks, and the various hours were made to correspond to the appropriate time of the day. Editorially, let me say that the result was more a better prayer-book for priests than a true resource for communal prayer.

Among the reforms of the cycle of feasts and seasons of the liturgical year, the renewed emphasis on Sunday as the principal day for celebrating the paschal mystery stands out.

Finally, provision was made for a more varied repertoire of liturgical music in line with *Sacrosanctum Concilium* 116.

The 1967 document *Musicam Sacram* was the first official document to sanction "appropriate songs" in addition to the various chants of the Mass printed in the Missal.

This list is incomplete since other factors played a role in the implementation of *Sacrosanctum Concilium*. But let us turn to the third part.

The Reception of the Reform and Where We Stand Today

As Cardinal Cupich said in his introduction to this series and as Ormond Rush and others have pointed out,[5] no interpretation of Vatican II can be complete without reflection on its reception. Needless to say, that remains a story in progress—a story so complex that I can make only a few observations here.

As I outlined in my book *Reforming the Liturgy: A Response to the Critics*,[6] some negative reaction to the reformed rites came quickly and vigorously in the wake of the reforms. This rejection took various forms: outright rejection of Vatican II itself, dissatisfaction with how the official rites corresponded to the council's mandates, and finally criticism of the implementation of the reformed rites in pastoral practice. On the other hand, the reformed rites were welcomed widely by a majority of Catholics. At the same time Mass attendance began to decrease significantly.

Critics of the reform—for example, Ross Douthat recently in the *New York Times* and George Weigel in the *Wall Street Journal*—attributed the decline to the reforms

[5] Ormond Rush, *The Vision of Vatican II: Its Fundamental Principles* (Collegeville, MN: Liturgical Press, 2019), 27–35; Faggioli, *Vatican II*, 6–11.

[6] John F. Baldovin, *Reforming the Liturgy: A Response to the* Critics (Collegeville, MN: Liturgical Press, 2008).

themselves.[7] In my opinion this is a flawed argument, *post hoc propter hoc* (i.e., "after this, therefore because of this"). One cannot demonstrate that a decline in Catholic practice was due to liturgical reforms. There is no necessary correlation between the decline in Mass attendance and the liturgical reforms. Rather it seems to me that the whole development of church life from the late 1950s onward witnessed a departure from a Catholicism marked by what I'll call the "fear factor." In other words, the fear of hell that had gripped Catholicism (and indeed Christianity itself) for so much of its history seems simply to have melted away.

In addition, I would speculate that the necessity of really engaging in the liturgical action—that is, full, conscious, and active participation—actually alienated many people from the liturgy. They were now forced to pay attention in a way that perhaps they had not done. More was required than simple attendance at the liturgy, and in fact the very accessibility of the liturgy revealed a number of flaws in its performance. This is perhaps somewhat cynical, but people found "better" ways to spend their Sunday mornings.

Suspicion of the post–Vatican II liturgical reform was aided by the attitudes of Cardinal Joseph Ratzinger / Pope Benedict XVI. In many of his writings, Pope Benedict made no secret of the fact that he considered the reform flawed, and he was identified with a group named the Reform of the Reform on issues like rejecting the practice of the priest facing the people during the liturgy, abandoning the new Eucharistic Prayers in favor of using only the old Roman Canon, and criticizing the nature of liturgical music.[8]

---

[7] Ross Douthat, "How Catholics Became Prisoners of Vatican II," *New York Times*, December 12, 2022; George Weigel, "What Vatican II Accomplished," *Wall Street Journal*, September 30, 2022.

[8] The literature here is voluminous. See, for example, Thomas Kocik, ed., *The Reform of the Reform? A Liturgy Debate: Reform or Return* (San Francisco: Ignatius Press, 2003); Neil Roy and Janet

Benedict has, of course, had a major impact on the progress of the reform. I find it hard to regard Benedict's 2007 *motu proprio*, *Summorum Pontificum*, which greatly expanded the use of the pre–Vatican II liturgy (which he named the "Extraordinary Form"), as anything less than troubling. Let me be clear, it was troubling not because it resurrected a form of the liturgy that was venerable and could indeed be beautifully celebrated, but rather because it implied a rejection of the entire baptismal ecclesiology of the council, a renewed vision of the church.

Among the various commentators on *Summorum Pontificum*, I find Georgia Masters Keightley very helpful.[9] She correctly identifies the ecclesiology of Vatican II, especially with regard to a pre–Vatican II understanding of the ministerial priesthood, as the central problem with Benedict's liberalization of permission to use the older rites. She illustrates the difficulty with this return to the pre–Vatican II liturgy in the loss of three important elements of the reformed Roman Rite liturgy of the Mass: the offertory procession, the prayers of the faithful, and the greeting of peace. All three of these features of the Mass of Paul VI accentuate the participation of the baptismal priesthood in celebrating the Eucharist.

In addition, as I have already mentioned, the revised rites for the sacraments (and at least in theory the Liturgy of the Hours) promote the participation of all the baptized into our celebrations. Let me cite just one example: the Baptism of Children. As the introduction to the rites of initiation

---

Rutherford, eds., *Benedict XVI and the Sacred Liturgy* (Portland, OR: Four Courts Press, 2010); Peter Kwasniewski, *The Once and Future Roman Rite: Returning to the Traditional Latin Liturgy after Seventy Years of Exile* (Gastonia, NC: Tan Books, 2022).

[9] Georgia Masters Keightley, "*Summorum Pontificum* and the Unmaking of the Lay Church," *Worship* 86, no.4 (July 2012): 290–310; see also John F. Baldovin, "Reflections on *Summorum Pontificum*," *Worship* 83, no. 2 (March 2009): 98–112.

makes clear, baptism is fundamentally a celebration of the church. Ideally the whole assembly participates in a baptism, and the parents and godparents are now active participants in their own right, instead of serving as ventriloquists for the child who cannot speak. The parents now affirm their own faith in taking responsibility for the upbringing of the child as a Christian.

As Pope Francis has made perfectly clear over the past two years with his decree *Traditionis Custodes* (basically overturning *Summorum Pontificum*), what Pope Benedict hoped would be an accommodation for those who love the older liturgy has now become a sign of division in the church, and more importantly, an expression of the rejection of the Second Vatican Council with its wholistic vision of church renewal.[10] This past summer, Pope Francis repeated his conviction, first found in article 1 of *Traditionis Custodes*, that the reformed liturgy is *the sole expression of the Lex Orandi of the Roman Rite*. In other words, we do not have two equal Catholic rites in today's Catholic Church but only one: the reformed rite after Vatican II. Such an outright and unprecedented contradiction of his predecessor should alert us to how very important it is to Pope Francis to support the current liturgical reform.

I could easily spend more time with the reaction to the reform, but in light of this book's subtitle, *Re-Energizing the Renewal,* I will move on to some concluding remarks.

Conclusion: What Now?

Let me remind you of the question asked by my colleague Paul DeClerck, with which I began this presentation: "How is it that after forty [now sixty] years we have still

[10] Francis, *Traditionis Custodes*, Apostolic Letter on the Use of the Roman Liturgy Prior to the Reform of 1970, July 16, 2021.

not helped people to understand that the liturgy is a truly communal event?"

I am convinced that the answer to Fr. DeClerck's question lies not so much in revising our new rites themselves. Of course, as with anything this side of God's reign, they are not perfect and they do require further inculturation—a topic I have bracketed for the sake of time. All the same, in my opinion they do represent a real step forward in our being the church, which of course means what it is to be a Christian, since there is no such thing as being a Christian without being a member of Christ's Body, the church.

The renewal of the rites themselves needs to be accompanied by a deeper renewal of our spiritual engagement in the liturgy. Among recent writers, the Italian scholar Andrea Grillo has made this point with particular force in his book *Beyond Pius V: Conflicting Interpretations of the Liturgical Reform.*[11] Of even greater significance is the fact that Pope Francis has called for the same kind of theological and spiritual renewal of the liturgy in this past summer's apostolic letter, *Desiderio Desideravi*, a letter on the importance of good liturgical celebration, or as it is called in Latin, the *ars celebrandi.*[12] In that letter Pope Francis did more than limit the use of the older pre–Vatican II rites. He called the church to a renewed appreciation of the spirit of the liturgy, the meaning of our participation in what Christ has done for us.

One aspect of this theological deepening, I would suggest, is the further work that needs to be done with regard to integrating a theology of the ordained priesthood with the baptismal ecclesiology that underlies *Sacrosanctum Concilium*. Another way of appreciating this baptismal

---

[11] Andrea Grillo, *Beyond Pius V: Conflicting Interpretations of the Liturgical Reform,* trans. Barry Hudock (Collegeville, MN: Liturgical Press, 2013).

[12] Francis, *Desiderio Desideravi*, Apostolic Letter on the Liturgical Formation of the People of God, June 29, 2022.

ecclesiology is the very synodal process of listening to one another in the Holy Spirit that Pope Francis has called us to.

There are of course many ongoing challenges with regard to our assimilation of the liturgical vision of the council. One more example: frequently one hears engaged couples asking why they need to get married in a church building. A beach in Monterey or a destination palazzo in Tuscany would be so much nicer. Questions like this show us how much work we have to do to help our people see that marriage is, as the *Catechism of the Catholic Church* states quite clearly, a sacrament in service of the church's communion. In other words, in addition to being a sacramental event that focuses on the couple and their families and friends, it is an event in which the church itself—*as church!*—participates in the very future of the human race.[13] We are not talking about theological niceties here, but about a vision of what it means to be members of the Body of Christ—the baptismal ecclesiology that undergirds the entirety of Vatican II. In addition, let us remember that Pope Francis is calling us to a profound appreciation of the beauty of the liturgy, which includes, of course, careful attention to liturgical music, our liturgical environment, and the style of our celebrations.

In conclusion, although some people assert that the post–Vatican II liturgical reform has been a failure, I believe that it has not been adequately tried; it has yet to be truly implemented. That is why this essay is titled "Reform in Motion."

[13] John Paul II, *Catechism of the Catholic Church*, 2nd ed. (Washington, DC: US Conference of Catholic Bishops, 2011), para. 1617, 1621, 1653.

4

Lumen Gentium, Synodality, and the Universal Call to Participation

Brian P. Flanagan

Reflecting on Jesus's post-Resurrection dialogue with Peter (John 21), on the sixtieth anniversary of the opening of the council on October 11, 2022, Pope Francis pointed to the love of and for the church that the council expressed.[1] He called us to return "to a Church madly in love with its Lord and with all the men and women whom he loves; to a Church that is rich in Jesus and poor in assets; to a Church that is free and freeing. This was the path that the Council pointed out to the Church."[2] In relation to the nature of the church and of our participation in it, what does the council, and particularly the Dogmatic Constitution on the Church,

[1] I am grateful to Sr. Maria Pascuzzi, CSJ, for her invitation to participate in this project, and to Holy Trinity Parish, Georgetown, its pastor Fr. Kevin Gillespie, SJ, and its pastoral associate for faith formation, Anne Marie Kaufmann, for welcoming me to share these ideas at the parish.

[2] Francis, Homily at the 60th Anniversary of the Beginning of the Second Vatican Ecumenical Council, October 11, 2022.

Lumen Gentium, teach us about how to love the church and how to love each other within the church? What does it teach us about church that is "free and freeing"?

This essay suggests that a major component of the conciliar renewal experienced over these past sixty years is the council's proclamation of how God's love for the entire people of God provides the foundation for a renewed theology of the dignity of each of the baptized, including the lay faithful who have always been the majority of the church. In its emphasis upon the metaphor of the church as the people of God, in the centrality given to baptism in the Constitution on the Sacred Liturgy, *Sacrosanctum Concilium*, and in its teaching on the universal call to holiness, *Lumen Gentium* renewed the church by repositioning our ordained leaders as servants to and with their fellow baptized servants of God, rather than like the "rulers of this world who lord it over them" (Matt 20:25). Much of the historic postconciliar renewal was based in this rediscovery of the real and active participation of the faithful in the liturgy, in mission, in evangelization, and in the pursuit of holiness.

And yet, at the same time, this renewal has remained incomplete. Most importantly, the council's theological teaching on the dignity and participation of all of the baptized faithful has not yet been adequately received in styles and structures of shared decision-making and discernment that would allow the lay faithful to exercise their rights and responsibilities as members of the church. In this way, Pope Francis's promotion of forms of synodality within the church, especially the ongoing worldwide Synod on Synodality currently in progress as of this writing, is best seen less as an innovation or a new direction, but instead as the necessary next step in the reception of the council's teaching on the church, in structures and deeds and not only in words.

The Baptized Faithful in *Lumen Gentium*

The Dogmatic Constitution on the Church (*Lumen Gentium*) is notable ecclesiologically for numerous reasons, including its opening to dialogue with other Christian churches, with the Jewish people, and with other religious traditions (LG 15–16); its reestablishment of the authority of the episcopate in relation to the pope (LG 18–27); and its reintroduction of an eschatological frame within which to understand the pilgrim church on its way to the fullness of God's reign (LG 48–51). But perhaps its major contribution to our understanding of the church is the revaluation of the dignity and calling of the baptized that runs throughout the text. That dignity is highlighted in three major ways: the emphasis upon the church as the people of God; the emphasis upon baptism as the sacrament by which the lay faithful participate in Christ's priestly, prophetic, and royal vocations; and the council's teaching on the universal call to holiness.

The story of the origins of *Lumen Gentium*'s second chapter, "The People of God," has often been told, precisely because of its centrality not only in the document but also in the history of the conciliar event. The conciliar decision to prioritize this chapter on the church as a whole over the subsequent chapter on the hierarchical offices of the church already points to the ecclesial revolution in the imaginations of the council fathers. In contrast to the draft schemas on the church with which they began the council, the final version of *Lumen Gentium* prioritizes the identity of the entire people of God as foundational for its understanding of the place and role of the hierarchy, rather than the hierarchy as foundational for an almost incidental laity. *Lumen*

Gentium puts the whole church "first," not because the laity are somehow better or more important than the clergy or religious, but simply to avoid the preconciliar common understanding that the reverse was true.

Beyond that location in the document, however, one can find in the content of *Lumen Gentium* 9–17 (chapter II, "People of God") as well as later in *Lumen Gentium* 30–38 (chapter IV, "The Laity") an emphasis on baptism as the constitutional sacrament of the church as the people of God. The council insists on the shared dignity and shared mission of all of the baptized as foundational to the different roles they exercise in the church. The council teaches, "In the church not everyone walks along the same path, yet all are called to holiness and have obtained an equal privilege of faith through the justice of God (see 2 Pet 1:1). Although by Christ's will some are appointed teachers, dispensers of the mysteries and pastors for the others, yet all the faithful enjoy a true equality with regard to the dignity and the activity which they share in the building up of the body of Christ" (LG 32). As Edward Hahnenberg has written, "It is the reclaiming of baptism that may very well be the greatest legacy of Vatican II's teaching on the laity."[3]

The council further teaches that by their baptism, all of the faithful participate in different ways in Christ's priestly, prophetic, and royal missions. While distinguishing the "common priesthood of the faithful" from the "ministerial or hierarchical priesthood" (LG 10), *Lumen Gentium* teaches that "the faithful indeed, by virtue of their royal priesthood, share in the offering of the Eucharist. They exercise that priesthood, too, by the reception of the sacraments, by prayer and thanksgiving, by the witness of a holy life, self-denial, and active charity" (LG 10). This reimagining

---

[3] Edward Hahnenberg, "Apostolate, Ministry, Mission: The Legacy of Vatican II's Teaching on the Laity," *Toronto Journal of Theology* 32 (2016): 238.

of the priestly participation of all of the baptized echoes the teaching of *Sacrosanctum Concilium* that "all the faithful should be led to take that full, conscious, and active part in liturgical celebrations which is demanded by the very nature of the liturgy" (SC 14).

Similarly with regard to their participation in Christ's prophetic office, *Lumen Gentium* teaches that the entire people of God "spreads abroad a living witness to him, especially by a life of faith and love and by offering to God a sacrifice of praise, the fruit of lips confessing his name" and that "the whole body of the faithful who have received an anointing which comes from the holy one cannot be mistaken in belief" (LG 12). Christ's prophetic office continues, *Lumen Gentium* teaches, "not only through the hierarchy who teach in his name and by his power, but also through the laity. He accordingly both establishes them as witnesses and provides them with an appreciation of the faith (*sensus fidei*) and the grace of the word" (LG 35). This baptismal call to prophetic evangelization and to participation in the teaching authority of the church, under the guidance of the hierarchy, is, as will be seen, foundational to the exercise of synodal structures of dialogue and shared discernment in the church.

The most fraught discussion in the text, however, revolves around the question of how, exactly, the laity participate in Christ's "kingly" office. Interestingly, chapter II on the people of God (LG 9–17) seems to omit the conversation entirely. In chapter IV, on the laity (LG 30–38), the focus returns to how lay Christians exercise their baptism in their responsibilities in the church and to the world. The latter is the dominant theme, as the council teaches that "the laity enjoy the principal role" in the church's mission to spread the reign of God more widely and more effectively in "the world," which is conceived as the laity's primary sphere of responsibility (LG 36). But in a second movement, one with deep implications for the place of synodality in ecclesiology, chapter IV discusses how the laity also participate, in a way appropriate to their role, in the governance of the church. As Amanda Osheim highlights, "Not only clergy and religious but all the baptized have responsibility for nurturing the life of the kingdom within the church."[4] The council's teaching on those roles bears citation at some length.

While always set within a wider context in which, "like all the faithful, the laity should promptly accept in Christian obedience what is decided by the pastors who, as teachers and rulers of the church, represent Christ" (LG 37), the council suggests an active involvement of all the Christian faithful in the shared governance of the church, as well as responsibilities of the clergy to receive their assistance:

> The laity should disclose their needs and desires to the pastors with that liberty and confidence which befits children of God and brothers and sisters in Christ. To the extent of their knowledge, competence or authority the laity are entitled, and indeed sometimes duty-bound, to express their opinion on matters which concern the good of the church. Should the occasion arise this should be done through the institutions established by the church for that purpose and always with truth, courage and prudence and with reverence and charity towards those who, by reason of their office, represent the person of Christ. (LG 37)

Similarly, when discussing the hierarchy's responsibilities with regard to lay involvement, the document states that "the sacred pastors, however, should recognize and promote the dignity and responsibility of the laity *in* the church

---

[4] Amanda C. Osheim, "The Christian Faithful," in *The Cambridge Companion to Vatican II*, ed. Richard Gaillardetz (Cambridge: Cambridge University Press, 2020), 211–31, at 224.

[emphasis added]. They should willingly use their prudent advice and confidently assign offices to them in the service of the church, leaving them freedom and scope for activity" (LG 37). The recurring language of "dignity" and "responsibility" suggests the baptismal foundation for these kingly/royal/governing responsibilities; as noted below, however, in the postconciliar reception the "institutions established by the church for that purpose" (LG 37) either failed to be established or were deeply hindered by both structural inadequacies and the lack of a conversion of ecclesial culture.

A third and final component of *Lumen Gentium*'s teaching on the participation of all the baptized in the work of Christ can be found in *Lumen Gentium*'s chapter V (LG 39–42), the council's inspirational—literally—rearticulation of the universal Call to Holiness. The council's teaching that "all Christians in whatever state or walk in life are called to the fullness of Christian life and to the perfection of charity" (LG 40) was, in the words of the late eminent historian John O'Malley, "the most remarkable aspect of *Lumen Gentium*."[5] As I have written elsewhere, the decision of the council to emphasize this theme of holiness in chapter V and beyond, and to emphasize the universality of that call rooted in baptism, may be one of the most important and often underestimated contributions of the council to our understanding of the church and the roles of the Christian faithful within it.[6]

This was a break with an entrenched "hierarchy of holiness" in which members of the clergy and those in the religious life had a "vocation to holiness" and in which the best that laypeople could do, mired as they were in the cares

---

[5] John O'Malley, *What Happened at Vatican II?* (Cambridge, MA: Belknap Press of Harvard University Press, 2008), 50–51.

[6] See Brian P. Flanagan, "The Universal Call to Holiness and Laity in the Church," *Toronto Journal of Theology* 32 (2016): 219–32.

of the world and family life, was hope to "avoid sin."[7] This text was rooted originally in drafts that focused upon the particular call to holiness and the evangelical counsels of those in religious life. But the final version reclaims the life of holiness as a baptismal vocation rather than a special vocation, and the chapter's location as a bridge between the document's treatments of the laity and of religious life help reimagine the distinct "walks in life" by which clergy, laity, and religious exercise their fundamental vocation to holiness in dialogue and complementarity. As John O'Malley wrote, "Holiness, the council thus said, is what the church is all about. This is an old truth, of course, and in itself is not remarkable. Yet no previous council had ever explicitly asserted this idea and certainly never developed it so repeatedly and at length."[8]

All three of these aspects of *Lumen Gentium*'s teaching, therefore—the emphasis on the shared mission of the members of the church as the people of God; the participation of all of the faithful in the threefold offices of Christ as priest, prophet, and king; and the universality of the vocation to holiness—helped the church reclaim baptism as the foundational sacrament of ecclesial order, rather than ordination. It has been widely reported that Pope St. John Paul II considered the day of his baptism, rather than the dates of his ordination or his installation as pope, as the most important day of his life.[9] Similarly, Pope Francis has repeatedly given Catholics a "homework assignment" to discover and celebrate the date of their own baptisms.[10] Such anecdotes illustrate well the council's crucial recovery

---

[7] See Aurelie Hagstrom, *The Emerging Laity: Vocation, Mission, and Spirituality* (New York: Paulist, 2010), 44.

[8] O'Malley, *What Happened at Vatican II?*, 51.

[9] See, for instance, George Weigel, "The Most Important Day of Your Life," *First Things*, April 27, 2016.

[10] See, for instance, Francis, General Audience, September 8, 2021.

of baptism as the sacramental dynamo that powers our participation in the life and mission of the church.

Reception of the Council

After the council, building upon the extensive lay apostolates and new religious communities that had developed in the first half of the twentieth century, the participation of all of the baptized Christian faithful in the life of the church grew enormously. Along with the revitalization and renewal of religious communities in relation to their founding charisms, the explosion of lay participation in liturgical, pastoral, evangelization, and social-service ministries in the postconciliar period across wide swaths of the Roman Catholic world marked a new way of being church together. What today seems "normal" in most Catholic spheres—lay people who work as pastoral associates, religious educators, lectors, ministers of the Eucharist, chaplains, and theologians—is a direct result of the renewal of the baptismal mission that began at the council.

Beyond this embrace of their participation in Christ's priestly and prophetic offices, however, the postconciliar church took some steps in establishing the structures and institutions called for in *Lumen Gentium* 37. At the parish and diocesan levels, the establishment of pastoral councils, of finance councils, and sometimes of more innovative forms of lay participation in the governance of their church all characterized attempts to dismantle a hierarchy in which the laity were expected only to pray, pay, and obey. The 1983 Code of Canon Law reaffirmed the institution of diocesan synods with wide participation (cc. 460–468), mandated diocesan (cc. 492–494) and parochial (c. 537) finance councils and a diocesan presbyteral council (cc. 495–502), and recommended the establishment of diocesan (cc. 511–514) and parochial (c. 536) pastoral councils. The Code of Canon Law also included a section on the rights and responsibilities of the Christian faithful, including the teaching of *Lumen Gentium* 37 that "in accord with the knowledge, competence, and preeminence which they possess, [the Christian faithful] have the right and even at times a duty to manifest to the sacred pastors their opinion on matters which pertain to the good of the Church," and even extending that teaching to include a right "to make their opinion known to the other Christian faithful" (c. 212, §3).

And yet despite these initiatives, the participation of all of the Christian faithful in shared discernment and decision-making in the church, that is, in their "kingly" vocation, has lagged behind their participation as priests and prophets. In many ways, the postconciliar church is still awaiting the "liberation of the laity" that Vatican II portended, with sometimes damaging and disappointing results.[11] This occurred for a number of reasons. For example, there were some issues with the institutions themselves. Only recommending pastoral councils, rather than requiring them, obviously limited their implementation. And the lack of transparency or accountability in the criteria for participation in these structures, often at the discretion of the appointing pastor or bishop, hindered their effectiveness and credibility. But at a deeper level, the lack of clarity about their role and of catechesis regarding how participation in ecclesial governance differed from the forms of participation found in modern electoral democracies was a more foundational weakness. As *Lumen Gentium* suggested and as the Code specified, the participation of the Christian faithful in ecclesial governance differed from forms of "one person, one vote" democracy with which many Catholics were familiar. As noted below, increasingly robust theologies of synodality

[11] The title of Paul Lakeland's important work is *The Liberation of the Laity: In Search of an Accountable Church* (New York: Continuum, 2004), see 192–205.

help to distinguish how important the consultative voice of the Christian faithful is for the leadership of their pastors, and yet the continuing presiding role of bishops and clergy within their communities distinguishes these forms of participation sharply from electoral democracy. This was compounded by an ongoing culture of clericalism and hierarchicalism, on the part of clergy and laity alike, that resisted any interruption of the norm that "Father knows best."

The result, therefore, was a bit like the introduction of democratic structures into a previously totalitarian society, in which the institutions "on the books" might have been well intended and even potentially useful but were hindered by the lack of a conversion of culture that would allow them to function well. Pastors at the parochial level and bishops at the diocesan level continued to act without the participation or consultation of the presbyterates and communities that they led, making decisions *for* them and not *with* them. This has led to an increasingly untenable situation in which all the faithful are called to full and active participation not only in the liturgy or in evangelization but in the shared governance of the church, but have no adequate structures or established culture in which to exercise these rights and responsibilities. Pope Francis's efforts to establish synodality as a central part of ecclesial identity, therefore, is not an innovation deriving sui generis from his papacy, but rather the fulfillment and the completion of Vatican II's teaching on the roles of all the baptized in Christ's kingly office. In this way, the promotion of synodality attempts to bring to completion one of the major unfinished projects begun at Vatican II.

Synodality

Austen Ivereigh has rightly said that the current Synod on Synodality may be "the biggest consultation exercise in human history."[12] Launched in September 2021, the process included consultations at the parish and diocesan levels, and will continue at the national, continental, and universal levels through two meetings of the synod in Rome in October 2023 and October 2024. Three aspects of this process seem to have stood out. First, such widespread consultation has produced a wide variety of documentation, including valuable reports from the ground in both diocesan and national syntheses and reports on consultations in religious communities, other Catholic institutions, and groups of Catholics with shared identities and interests.[13] In all of this documentation, one can get a snapshot of some of the "joys and hopes, griefs and sorrows" of Catholics around the world at this point in history. Second, one can find in the content of these consultations some remarkable convergences for such a diverse group of over 1.3 billion people. Particularly in relation to issues of clerical sexual abuse, the status of women in the church, the decline in participation of young people, and outreach to Catholics on the margins of ecclesial life, these documents show some of the shared concerns of Catholics throughout the world. Yet they also give the impression, particularly in some already polarized Catholic communities like that of the United States, of a lack

---

[12] Quoted in Inés San Martín, "Experts See Synodality as 'Biggest Consultation Exercise in Human History,' " Crux Online, October 11, 2011.

[13] See, for instance, the remarkable National Synthesis of the People of God in the United States of America for the Diocesan Phase of the 2021-2023 Synod, https://www.usccb.org/resources/us-national-synthesis-2021-2023-synod. General Secretariat of the Synod, "Enlarge the Space of Your Tent—The Working Document for the Continental Stage," October 2022, https://www.synod.va/content/dam/synod/common/phases/continental-stage/dcs/Documento-Tappa-Continentale-EN.pdf; and General Secretariat of the Synod, *Instrumentum Laboris* for the First Session, October 2023, https://www.synod.va/content/dam/synod/common/phases/universal-stage/il/ENG_INSTRUMENTUM-LABORIS.pdf.

of agreement on how to move forward together, especially in relation to some of the most controversial issues. Third, in some circles, especially those already suspicious of Pope Francis's change in tone and style with regard to welcoming those on the ecclesial margins, the synod has been met with outright suspicion and ridicule in some cases, and superficial participation or disengagement in others.

And while there are many causes for the unevenness of synodal participation and response, at least one problematic aspect of the continuing synod is the lack of a shared understanding of synodality and its place in the life of the church. This is expressed from some perspectives as suspicion or critique, often under the rhetorical slogan that "the church is not a democracy." In other cases, the synodal process has been embraced, but treated by some Catholics as something like either a form of participatory democracy or, more often, a slightly more spiritual form of strategic planning. These misunderstandings point to the need to recover a shared sense of what synodality actually is, how it has functioned and might function in the church, and how it differs from other forms of participatory discernment with which many Catholics have more experience. Such an understanding, coming directly from the theology of the role of the baptized faithful in the church outlined at Vatican II, and Pope Francis's current efforts to form a more synodally governed church, should be seen as a continuing act of reception of the church's teaching on the universal call to holiness of all the faithful of the church.

Historically, synods and synodality were among the dominant forms of ecclesial decision-making in the history of Christianity. The so-called Synod of Jerusalem[14] described

[14] Often called the "council of Jerusalem," the text of Acts 15, as underlined recently by the International Theological Commission, shows that it was not only a "council" of the leaders of the church, those whom our bishops and pastors succeed in the modern Catholic

in Acts 15 became the idealized example of shared synodal discernment in the church, and in the centuries that followed, decision-making done through shared discernment became the dominant form of ecclesial governance. Even after the rise of the mono-episcopate, bishops meeting in council were thought to exercise their role with and on behalf of their local churches, rather than monarchically set above those churches. Indeed, in the most centralized or monarchical moments of episcopal and papal governance, the idea of shared discernment remained a touchstone of Catholic practice—the Catholic Church's teaching on papal authority and infallibility were defined, in fact, at and by a council, not as an act of papal fiat. Given this history, synodality is arguably the most traditional form of ecclesial governance in Christianity, despite its relative desuetude in recent centuries of Catholic experience.

The roles of leaders and of all the baptized in synodality follow from synodality's origins as an outgrowth of the sacramental definition of the church, the *ekklēsia* or assembly, when gathered to discern a path forward in the face of a new challenge or opportunity. The church-as-assembly, gathered to hear the Scriptures and break the bread in its eucharistic practice, extended that presence when it continued that assembly to make decisions or respond to crises. And, as in its eucharistic practice, the distinctive roles and relationships of individuals within that assembly were determined sacramentally. Where synodal forms of discernment, like the postconciliar liturgical reforms, most differed from the practice of the immediately preceding centuries is that synodal forms of discernment restore baptism as the

Church, but included the active presence and participation of the entire church of Jerusalem, making "synod of Jerusalem" a better and more expansive title for the event. See International Theological Commission, "Synodality in the Life and Mission of the Church," March 2, 2018, especially nos. 20–22.

sacramental engine powering our shared participation in both the liturgy and the church's governance. Thus, when the church-as-assembly gathers for Eucharist, "Everyone plays an active part, though with varied roles and contributions,"[15] in the words of the International Theological Commission (ITC). Ordination, while a crucial aspect of the order of relationships that define the roles and the responsibilities by which we live out our baptismal vocation, is no longer seen as the font from which either liturgical participation or participation in ecclesial governance flow. Rather, baptism returns to its proper place as the starting point upon which all of our forms of ecclesial participation are based. In the words of the ITC,

> Synodality means that the whole Church is a subject and that everyone in the Church is a subject. The faithful are σύνοδοι, companions on the journey. They are called to play an active role inasmuch as they share in the one priesthood of Christ (LG 10) and are meant to receive the various charisms given by the Holy Spirit in view of the common good (LG 12 and 32). Synodal life reveals a Church consisting of free and different subjects, united in communion, which is dynamically shown to be a single communitarian subject built on Christ, the corner-stone, and on the Apostles, who are like pillars, built like so many living stones into "a spiritual house" (cf. 1 Peter 2:5), "a dwelling-place of God in the Spirit" (Ephesians 2:22).[16]

This sacramental foundation distinguishes synodal forms of shared discernment from other forms of decision-making in our world, and also explains some of its particularity. Unlike the one-person, one-vote forms of participatory

[15] "Synodality in the Life and Mission of the Church," no. 21.
[16] "Synodality in the Life and Mission of the Church," no. 55.

democracy that we are used to in our political life, synodality extends the sacramental order of the particular roles, duties, charisms, and responsibilities of "all," "some," and "one" in our differentiated participation.[17] To the frustration of some Catholics, synodality is not a form of lightly baptized democratic practice, but a different kind of politics altogether. And yet, at the same time, synodality differs from the forms of entirely monarchical, top-down lines of power and authority that constituted such a dominant form of historic European political structures and can be found in many corporate businesses today. In synodality, "bosses," if such is even the right word, are expected to consult widely and listen carefully, not simply as a "best practice" but out of respect for the baptismal dignity of all of the members of the church.

What is at stake, therefore, is not whether synodal practices should be sacramentally ordered, but which sacraments do the ordering. According to the report in "Enlarge the Space of Your Tent," what emerged from all of the national documents is "a profound re-appropriation of the common dignity of all the baptized," which is, in the words of the document, "the authentic pillar of a synodal church."[18] Recurring reference to the baptismal dignity of all of the Christian faithful in many of the synodal documents thus far suggests that their authors are aware of this movement toward a more synodal church as the completion of a trajectory that, beginning in *Lumen Gentium*, strives to renew our understanding of baptism as the constitutive sacrament that gives individuals their place in the assembly of the church. While we have been operating for some centuries under the mistaken idea that ecclesial identity and governance flows from our ordained pastors, a synodal church has recovered the council's insight into a more traditional ecclesiology

---

[17] Cf. "Synodality in the Life and Mission of the Church," no. 64.

[18] "Enlarge the Space of Your Tent," no. 9.

in which our ecclesial identity, our participation in the Eucharist, and our participation in the shared governance of our church is rooted in baptism. In this way, we can see that the "full and active participation" in the liturgy of all of the baptized leads to the "full and active participation" in the life of the church of all of the baptized. By incarnating in new structures and forms the council's teaching on the participation of all of the baptized in Christ's priestly, prophetic, *and* royal offices, the synodal church that we are now beginning to recover should be seen as a delayed, and yet essential, act of reception of the council's teaching on the dignity of the baptized.

5

Dei Verbum and the Roots of Synodality

Ormond Rush

Synodality has been called, if not the *central* theme, then certainly one of the most emphasized themes of Pope Francis's pontificate. In preparation for the forthcoming sessions of the Synod of Bishops, it is clearly evident from the responses of dioceses throughout the world that the vast majority of Catholics have found the vision of a synodal church refreshing and liberating. According to Pope Francis, a "synodal church" would be, in every dimension of its life, he says, "a church which listens."[1] Ultimately, this ecclesial listening means listening to the enlightenment of God's Holy Spirit, the one who, Jesus promised, will always guide the church toward the fulness of truth.[2] And, the church is listening to the Holy Spirit if and when it listens to, and discerns, the Spirit speaking within the hearts of all

[1] Francis, Address for the Commemoration of the 50th Anniversary of the Institution of the Synod of Bishops, October 17, 2015.

[2] John 16:13: "But when he comes, the Spirit of truth, he will guide you to all truth."

the baptized—lay and ordained—to whom the Spirit has given what the Dogmatic Constitution on the Church, *Lumen Gentium*, calls "the entire people's supernatural sense of the faith" (LG 12).

The notion of synodality has, however, had its harsh critics, as you would well know. Moreover, claims that the pope's vision has its roots in Vatican II have also been rebutted. For example, Archbishop Charles Chaput, in an interview recently about the Synod on Synodality, has remarked, "The claim that Vatican II somehow implied the need for synodality as a permanent feature of Church life is simply false. The council never came close to suggesting that."[3]

In my presentation, I propose—to the contrary—that Pope Francis's vision on synodality has deep roots in the vision of Vatican II. Certainly, the terms "synodality" and "synodal" (and, I might add, the term "collegiality") are not part of the Latin vocabulary used in the documents of Vatican II. When they do speak of "synods," it is in reference to bishops collaborating more closely, in an act of episcopal collegiality, one of the great themes of Vatican II. Nevertheless, many of the themes that the words "synodality" and "synodal" evoke can indeed be grounded in both the vigorous debates during Vatican II and then in its final sixteen documents. As one bishop has summarized it: synodality refers to, "not some of the bishops some of the time, but all of the Church all of the time."[4]

As I have said on other occasions, "Synodality is Vatican II in a nutshell."[5] Many elements of the council's multifac-

---

[3] See "Chaput: 'Speaking the Truth Is Polarizing,'" *The Pillar*, January 13, 2023.

[4] Archbishop Mark Coleridge, "From Wandering to Journeying: Thoughts on a Synodal Church," *Australasian Catholic Record* 93, no. 3 (July 2016): 340–50, at 348.

[5] Nathalie Becquart, "Like Vatican II, the Synod Is a Dynamic

eted vision could be mentioned, elements that situate the council's great doctrine of collegiality on a much broader ecclesial canvas. Let me list some of them:

1. The participation of all the baptized in the mission of the church.
2. The participation of all the baptized, not just the hierarchy, in the so-called three offices of Christ: the prophetic office, that is, the teaching office of the church; the priestly office, that is, the sanctifying office of the church; and the kingly office, that is, the governing office of the church.
3. The notion of the local church as the Catholic Church fully in that place.
4. The notion of "communion" between all these local churches, and of the Catholic Church as a communion of churches.
5. The call for dialogue, not only with other Christians, with other religions, and with unbelievers, but first and foremost, dialogue within the church, not only within a local church, but also between all the local churches that make up the church catholic.
6. The dignity of the human person, of their *sensus fidei*, of their charisms, and of their conscience.

I could happily expand on each of those points of Vatican II's overall vision, and I will certainly touch on some of them again in this presentation. But my given task is to reflect on *Dei Verbum*, the council's Dogmatic Constitution on Divine Revelation. So, beyond those elements of the council's overall vision I have just mentioned, I hope to show that *Dei Verbum* especially presents teachings that are fundamental for understanding what it means to be "a church which listens," and dialogues, and discerns.

Example of the Church in History," *America*, April 2023.

For this essay I have selected just three clusters of teachings in *Dei Verbum*—on revelation, on faith, and on tradition. Along the way, I refer to other documents of Vatican II that relate to these topics; this procedure simply follows a principle of interpretation called "inter-textuality": applied to the sixteen documents of Vatican II, that means each document is to be interpreted in the light of the other fifteen.

Revelation: Divine Revelation as an Ongoing Divine-Human Dialogue

Let us begin with what I believe is one of the most important shifts taken at Vatican II. Well, it was not so much a shift as a retrieval of an understanding from the Bible and the early church: that is, "divine revelation" is to be understood, primarily, as the divine offer of a lifelong covenant friendship-relationship with the God who has created us. And, secondarily, from that relationship, through time there comes a communication of knowledge about God and God's will for humankind; this is the content God reveals within the divine-human relationship.

Official Catholic theology on the eve of Vatican II saw divine revelation almost exclusively in this second sense, but in a very restricted understanding of this second sense. So, to understand how important the council's retrieval was, it is helpful to examine briefly the so-called neoscholastic theology that predominated in the centuries before Vatican II, especially in the early twentieth century and leading up to the council. It is striking that for many of the current critics of synodality, as I am hearing them, this neoscholastic theology is what they are still hankering for. It was a theology that had a predominantly one-dimensional view of revelation, what could be called "verbal-propositionalist." Here, *revelation is seen only as a catechism of doctrines, which are to be understood as God's eternal thoughts and words, expressed in timeless propositions*. An important corollary of this is: it is the magisterium alone that has authority over the interpretation of these doctrines.

I used the word "one-dimensional." This model of revelation is certainly one key dimension that can be found throughout the Bible, where we see God speaking, often through intermediaries, such as the prophets or Jesus. For example, in the opening sentence of the Letter to the Hebrews, we read, "In times past, God spoke in partial and various ways to our ancestors through the prophets; in these last days, he spoke to us through a son, whom he made heir of all things" (Heb 1:1–2).

However, reacting against a restricted understanding of "God speaking," mid-twentieth-century revivals in the various disciplines of theology retrieved other aspects of the biblical witness and of writers from the patristic period. Drawing on this so-called *ressourcement* scholarship, *Dei Verbum* brings these to the fore and presents a much richer view of divine revelation, and of the way God relates to human beings along the paths of history. Without in any way rejecting the importance of the verbal-propositionalist dimension, two other dimensions of divine revelation are foregrounded in the first chapter of *Dei Verbum*; they could be called the relational-personalist dimension and the sacramental dimension.

First, regarding the relational-personalist dimension, let me quote the passage in *Dei Verbum*'s first chapter, with the title "On Revelation Itself":

> It pleased God, in his goodness and wisdom, to reveal himself and to make known the mystery of his will (see Eph 1:9), which was that people can draw near to the Father, through Christ, the Word made flesh, in the holy Spirit, and thus become sharers in the divine nature (see Eph 2:18; 2 Pet 1:4). By this revelation, then, the invisible God (see Col 1:15; 1 Tim 1:17), from the fullness of his love, addresses men and women as his

friends (see Ex 33:11; Jn 15:14–15), and lives among them (see Bar 3:38), in order to invite and receive them into his own company. (DV 2)

Here, the event of revelation is God revealing God's very self. God's loving and merciful heart is laid bare. *Indeed, the God who has created us wants to love us and to be friends with us*. Every believer has the possibility of such an intimate relationship with the God who has created them. This intimate offer is extended to all, and not just to a select few, such as popes and bishops. Vatican II elsewhere, in the Pastoral Constitution on the Church in the Modern World, *Gaudium et Spes*, speaks of this possibility of relationship with God as the very ground of the dignity of the human person: "Human dignity rests above all on the fact that humanity is called to communion with God [*ad communionem cum Deo*]. The invitation to converse with God [*ad colloquium cum Deo*] is addressed to men and women as soon as they are born" (GS 19). In other words, through God's self-revelation, we are invited "to converse with God."

Second, regarding the sacramental dimension of revelation, let me quote the passage that follows directly from the one before, from *Dei Verbum* 2: "The pattern (*oeconomia*) of this revelation unfolds through deeds and words which are intrinsically connected: the works performed by God in the history of salvation show forth and confirm the doctrine and realities signified by the words; the words, for their part, proclaim the works, and bring to light the mystery they contain" (DV 2).

The focus here, deliberately, is not just on God's words, but also on how God acts and relates to human beings. Later, in its fourth chapter devoted to the Old Testament, *Dei Verbum* 14 states, "[God] acquired a people for himself, and to them he revealed himself in words and deeds as the one, true, living God (*se tamquam unicum Deum verum et vivum verbis ac gestis revelavit*)." In other words, as Brian

Daley observes, "*Dei Verbum* treats revelation as a verbal noun, an activity of the ever mysterious and ever-present God in human history, rather than as a body of information to be studied."[6] Christoph Theobald calls this a "sacramental conception of revelation."[7]

In other words, divine revelation did not just happen two thousand years or so ago, when Jesus went about his ministry, was killed, rose from the dead, appeared, and sent the Holy Spirit. God's self-revelation (always in Christ, through the Holy Spirit) and God's offer of relationship, is a living reality here and now. That does not mean there can be some new revelation, beyond what the Scripture has witnessed to, and tradition asserts. But the same God, in the same Jesus Christ, through the enlightenment and empowerment of the same Holy Spirit, is forever engaging and conversing with human beings in the ever-new here and now of history that relentlessly moves humanity into new perceptions, new questions, and new insights, in diverse cultures and places, especially in his church, as it courses into an unknown future until the eschaton.

Vatican II, accordingly, urged the church to be ever attentive to the movements of God present in the flow of history, by attending to "the signs of the times" (GS 4, 11). Discernment of the signs of the times seeks to determine what God is urging us to see in new times, but also urging

---

[6] Brian E. Daley, "Knowing God in History and in the Church: *Dei Verbum* and '*Nouvelle Théologie*,' " in *Ressourcement: A Movement for Renewal in Twentieth-Century Catholic Theology*, ed. Gabriel Flynn and Paul D. Murray (Oxford: Oxford University Press, 2012), 333–51, at 347.

[7] Christoph Theobald, "The Church under the Word of God," in *History of Vatican II*, vol. 5, *The Council and the Transition: The Fourth Period and the End of the Council, September 1965–December 1965*, ed. Giuseppe Alberigo and Joseph A. Komonchak, trans. Matthew J. O'Connell (Maryknoll, NY: Orbis Books, 2006), 275–362, at 345.

us to be attentive to the traps—where we could be being drawn into ways of thinking that are not "of God." These traps could lie in being anchored, mindlessly, in the past, or mindlessly in the present.

Discerning the difference between opportunities and traps is the task of all the faithful—laity, bishops, and theologians—everyone, as *Gaudium et Spes* teaches: "With the help of the holy Spirit, it is the task of the whole people of God, particularly of its pastors and theologians, to listen to and distinguish the many voices of our times and to interpret them in the light of God's Word, in order that the revealed truth may be more deeply penetrated, better understood, and more suitably presented" (GS 44).

These personalist and sacramental dimensions of revelation require a reconfiguration and reframing of the ever-important verbal-propositionalist dimension, the aspect of revelation as "a body of information to be studied," to use Brian Daley's phrase. This verbal-propositionalist model relates to the highly important issue of the content of revelation. The passage before, from *Dei Verbum* 2, speaks of God not only revealing God's very self, but also making known new perspectives on "the mystery of God's will." Then, *Dei Verbum* 6 brings together both notions—God's personal self-communication and the communication of content: "By divine revelation God wished to manifest and communicate both himself and the eternal decrees of his will concerning the salvation of humankind." In the next two sections we explore further the need for interrelating these two aspects.

But for now, how is all this relevant to synodality? If, as Brian Daly summarizes it, revelation is the "activity of the ever-mysterious and ever-present God in human history," then interpretation of revelation is not only about attending to something that happened in the past, but also attending to what God is making known in the present, in Christ through the Holy Spirit. Synodality emphatically brings to the fore this key insight, especially the role of the Spirit in facilitating the divine-human encounter of revelation. But let me pause on that one for the moment. I first need to speak of other themes, such as faith and its necessary location in time, that is, in history.

Faith: The Holy Spirit and Participatory Knowledge of God

From *Dei Verbum*'s personalist dimension of God's self-revelation comes a corresponding personalist dimension of the human response to that divine outreach—faith. In *Dei Verbum* 5, faith is first defined simply as "our response to God who reveals." Just as revelation is presented as God seeking a loving friendship-relationship with human beings, so too faith is presented as a response that seeks, in return, a loving friendship-relationship with God. This is faith as "believing"; it is more a verb than a noun. Then, a second sense of faith emerges out of the first sense: that is, assenting to the content of the truths God communicates. *Dei Verbum* 5 describes together these two dimensions of faith as both a believing relationship and as the acceptance of, or assent to, the content of faith that this relationship communicates. It states, "By faith one freely commits oneself entirely to God, making 'the full submission of intellect and will to God who reveals,' and willingly assenting to the revelation given by God."

Then, the role of the Holy Spirit in faith is emphasized. The Holy Spirit both opens the hearts of believers to God's loving outreach, and also helps them to understand, interpret, and apply in their lives their friendship-relationship with God, as well as understand the implications of the content of revelation: "For this faith to be accorded we need the grace of God, anticipating it and assisting it, as well as the interior helps of the holy Spirit, who moves the heart and converts it to God, and opens the eyes of the mind and 'makes it easy for all to accept and believe the truth.' The same holy Spirit constantly perfects faith by his gifts, so that revelation may be more and more deeply understood" (DV 5). Later, in *Dei Verbum* 8, there will be an allusion to the Holy Spirit granting to believers not only the gift of faith but also a "sense of the faith" or "sense for the faith." This capacity enables believers to discern what God would want of us in the nitty-gritty of our daily life and relationships. But I speak more later on this "sense of the faith" (or *sensus fidei*), on how all the baptized have this capacity, and on its relevance for a listening, synodal church. Here we need to explore a bit more this personalist-relational dimension of faith.

In *Dei Verbum* 2, we read that, through believing and their faith-relationship with God, believers become "sharers in the divine nature" (citing Eph 2:18 and 2 Pet 1:4).[8] Through this relationship, we are told, God seeks "to invite and receive them into his own company" (DV 2). This citation of 2 Peter 1:4, on becoming "sharers in the divine nature," alludes to the notion of "participation" in the very life of God, and what Greek patristic theologians called "*theosis*," that is, a process of "divinization," becoming one with God.[9] Through it, believers can not only participate

[8] Eph 2:17–18: "[Christ Jesus] came and preached peace to you who were far off and peace to those who were near, for through him we both *have access in one Spirit to the Father*." 2 Pet 1:4: "Through these, he has bestowed on us the precious and very great promises, so that through them you may *come to share in the divine nature*, after escaping from the corruption that is in the world because of evil desire."

[9] Michael J. Thate, Kevin J. Vanhoozer, and Constantine R. Campbell, eds., *"In Christ" in Paul: Explorations in Paul's Theology of Union and Participation* (Grand Rapids: Wm. B. Eerdmans, 2018). See also Michael J. Christensen and Jeffery A. Wittung, eds., *Partakers of the Divine Nature: The History and Development of Deification*

in the divine life but, through that participation, they have access to a particular kind of intimate knowledge of God and insight into the mystery of God's will.

Later, in its second chapter on the transmission of revelation and faith, *Dei Verbum* 8 goes on to speak of this experiential aspect of faith, when it names one way in which faith is lived and passed on, on the basis of what could be called believers' "lived faith" (and I quote here from the Vatican website translation): "This tradition which comes from the Apostles develops in the Church with the help of the Holy Spirit. For there is a growth in the understanding of the realities and the words which have been handed down. This happens through. . . ." Then the text goes on to list three ways through which the Holy Spirit leads the church to growth in understanding the realities and words being handed down: (1) theological scholarship, (2) the applied faith of believers, and (3) the oversight of the magisterium. The second means is (and I quote) "a penetrating understanding of the spiritual realities which [believers] experience." In other words, all believers have the capacity for this "penetrating understanding," not just popes and bishops.

While the phrase *sensus fidei* is not specifically used, most commentators see here a direct reference to believers' *sensus fidei* ("sense of the faith"), to which *Lumen Gentium* 12 and other passages in the Vatican II documents give such high doctrinal significance. The passage from *Lumen Gentium* 12 is one of Pope Francis's favorite Vatican II quotes. It states,

> The holy people of God shares also in Christ's prophetic office . . . (*universitas fidelium*) who have received an anointing which comes from the holy one (see 1 Jn 2:20 and 27) cannot be mistaken in belief (*in credendo*

---

in the Christian Traditions (Grand Rapids: Baker Academic, 2007); Paul M. Collins, *Partaking in Divine Nature: Deification and Communion* (New York: T & T Clark, 2010).

> *falli nequit*). It shows this characteristic through the entire people's supernatural sense of the faith (*mediante supernaturali sensu fidei totius populi*), when, "from the bishops to the last of the faithful," it manifests a universal consensus in matters of faith and morals. By this sense of the faith (*sensus fidei*), aroused and sustained by the Spirit of truth, the people of God, guided by the sacred magisterium which it faithfully obeys, receives not the word of human beings, but truly the word of God (see 1 Thess 2:13), "the faith once for all delivered to the saints" (Jude 3). The people unfailingly adheres to this faith, penetrates it more deeply through right judgment, and applies it more fully in daily life.

This intimate sense of God, and of God's will, is not necessarily some perfect and finely articulated sense that is formulated in the sophisticated categories of theology. Rather, it is more "a sixth sense," an intuition that expresses knowledge more akin to the knowing between lovers or between friends. This fuzzy but real nature of *sensus fidei* is neatly captured in the perspective of Jewish theologian Rabbi Abraham Heschel, when he writes of the Jewish prophets' sense of God: "The prophets had no theory or 'idea' of God. What they had was an *understanding*. Their God understanding was not the result of a theoretical inquiry, of a groping in the midst of alternatives about the being and attributes of God. To the prophets, God was overwhelmingly real and shatteringly present. They never spoke of Him as from a distance. They lived as witnesses. . . . They disclosed attitudes *of* God, rather than ideas *about* God."[10] You will recall that *Lumen Gentium* 12's teaching on "the entire people's supernatural sense of the faith"

[10] Abraham J. Heschel, "The Theology of Pathos," in *The Prophets* (New York: Harper & Row, 1962), 221–31, at 221 (emphasis in original).

comes within its discussion of the so-called prophetic office of Christ, that is, the teaching office of the church.

How is all this relevant to synodality? A synodal church seeks to tap into this experiential knowledge of believers as they apply the Gospel in their lives. All believers—all those who respond in faith to their Creator God reaching out to them in love and friendship—have an "access" to God that has a significant ecclesial authority when it comes to knowing the mystery of God's will—for today. Therefore, as Pope Francis urges, "Let us trust in our People, in their memory and in their 'sense of smell,' let us trust that the Holy Spirit acts in and with our People and that this Spirit is not merely the 'property' of the ecclesial hierarchy."[11]

Elsewhere, commenting on that passage from *Lumen Gentium* 12 on "the supernatural *sensus fidei* of the whole people," the pope states, "The *sensus fidei* prevents a rigid separation between an '*ecclesia docens*' [a teaching church] and an '*ecclesia discens*' [a learning church], since the flock likewise has *an instinctive ability to discern the new ways that the Lord is revealing to the Church.*"[12] Therefore, through listening to the *sensus fidei* of the people of God—that is, the *sensus fidelium*—the church is seeking to listen to the Spirit of God, since the Spirit's instrument of communication is the *sensus fidei* given, along with faith, to all the baptized. "A synodal Church is a Church which listens. . . . The faithful people, the college of bishops, the Bishop of Rome: all listening to each other, and all listening to the Holy Spirit."[13]

[11] Francis, Letter to Cardinal Ouellet, March 19, 2016.

[12] Francis, "Address of His Holiness, Pope Francis. Ceremony Commemorating the 50th Anniversary of the Institution of the Synod of Bishops," October 17, 2015, https://www.vatican.va/content/francesco/en/speeches/2015/october/documents/papa-francesco_20151017_50-anniversario-sinodo.html.

[13] Francis, 50th anniversary of the institution of the Synod of Bishops, 2015.

Tradition: The Holy Spirit, Ongoing Dialogue with God throughout History, and "Living Tradition"

In the third section of my presentation, we now come to the topic of "tradition." How "tradition" is understood depends on how "revelation" and "faith" are being understood. The topic of tradition was by far the most contentious issue in the debates and drafting of *Dei Verbum*. Throughout his commentary on those debates, Joseph Ratzinger says that there were basically two different approaches to tradition, characterizing, respectively, the minority and the majority among the bishops. He calls them a "static" understanding of tradition and a "dynamic" understanding.[14] The former is legalistic and propositionalist; the latter is personalist and sacramental.

One of the great achievements of Vatican II is its teaching on episcopal collegiality. The bishops, like the early apostles, constitute a "college," a body that has oversight of the community's life. As the Scripture scholars among you would know, there is no univocal meaning in the New Testament given to that word "apostle"; one could highlight, for example, the different notions of "apostle" in the writings of Paul, Luke, and John. *Dei Verbum* does well to use the vague designation "those apostles and others associated with them" (DV 7), or "the apostles . . . and others of the apostolic age" (DV 18). Even the timeline of "the apostolic age" is somewhat vague. What is clear is that, for *Dei Verbum*, the New Testament is understood as encapsulating a dynamic tradition process that was at work in the years after the resurrection and Pentecost. Even within the first

[14] Joseph Ratzinger, "Chapter II: The Transmission of Divine Revelation," in *Commentary on the Documents of Vatican II*, vol. 3, ed. Herbert Vorgrimler (New York: Herder, 1969), 181–98.

generations after the death of Jesus, the apostles and their companions are remembering differently the words of Jesus and adapting "the Gospel" to the context of their hearers, or as *Dei Verbum* 19 expresses it, "explained with an eye to the situation of the churches (*statui ecclesiarum attendendo*)."

The "apostolic tradition" is therefore a "living tradition" that the church must emulate. *Dei Verbum* uses this precise phrase in article 12. Earlier, in *Dei Verbum* 8, while the precise phrase is not used, the whole article describes tradition as a living process that involves the whole church and its whole life. "What was handed on by the apostles comprises everything that serves to make the people of God live their lives in holiness and increase their faith. In this way the church, in its doctrine, life and worship, perpetuates and transmits to every generation all that it itself is, all that it believes" (DV 8).

Then in the next paragraph it speaks of those three factors (mentioned earlier) through which the Holy Spirit guides the church and assists in the development of the apostolic tradition throughout history: "This tradition which comes from the Apostles develops in the Church with the help of the Holy Spirit. For there is a growth in the understanding of the realities and the words which have been handed down. This happens through. . . ." And then the text goes on to list those three ways through which the Holy Spirit leads the church to growth in understanding of the realities and words being handed down: theological scholarship, the applied faith of believers, and the oversight of the magisterium. In other words, within the church, there is to be a dialogue between these three factors: theological scholarship, the *sensus fidelium*, and the magisterium. Joseph Ratzinger's commentary on this passage is telling:

> It is important that the progress of the word [of God] in the time of the Church is not seen simply as a function of the hierarchy, but is anchored in the whole life

> of the church; through it, we hear in what is said that which is unsaid. The whole spiritual experience of the Church, its believing, praying and loving intercourse with the Lord and his word, causes our understanding of the original truth to grow and in the today of faith extracts anew from the yesterday of its historical origin what was meant for all time and yet can be understood only in the changing ages and in the particular way of each. In this process of understanding, which is the concrete way in which tradition proceeds in the Church, the work of the teaching office is one component (and, because of its nature, a critical one, not a productive one), but it is not the whole.[15]

To emphasize the importance of the involvement of the whole people in maintaining the faith with fidelity throughout the centuries, Joseph Ratzinger might well have quoted now-saint John Henry Newman when writing about the failure of many of the bishops after the Council of Nicaea to maintain the belief in the full divinity of Christ, as proclaimed in the Nicene Creed. In the 1871 third edition of his book *The Arians of the Fourth Century*, Newman added an appendix, which, in effect, summarizes the thesis of his whole historical study of the Arian crisis. Titled "The Orthodoxy of the Body of the Faithful during the Supremacy of Arianism," the appendix begins, "The episcopate, whose action was so prompt and concordant at Nicaea on the rise of Arianism, did not, as a class or order of men, play a good part in the troubles consequent upon the Council, and the laity did. The Catholic people, in the length and breadth of Christendom, were the obstinate champions of Catholic truth, and the bishops were not."[16]

---

[15] Ratzinger, "Chapter II: The Transmission of Divine Revelation," 186.

[16] John Henry Newman, *The Arians of the Fourth Century*, 3rd

This living tradition, by which the whole church continues its work in every age throughout history, is a dialogue mediated by the Holy Spirit. At the end of *Dei Verbum* 8, we read the following statement, which raises the question of how the church today might maintain this faithful dialogue between God and the whole church: "Thus, as the centuries go by, the church is always advancing towards the plenitude of divine truth, until eventually the words of God are fulfilled in it. . . . Thus God, who spoke in the past, continues to converse (*colloquitur*) with the spouse of his beloved Son. And the Holy Spirit, through whom the living voice of the Gospel rings out in the church—and through it in the world—leads believers to the full truth and makes the word of Christ dwell in them in all its richness."

Conclusion: How Is All This Relevant to Synodality?

First, with his notion of synodality, Pope Francis is attempting to bring a fully Trinitarian balance to our Catholic understanding of how the church maintains fidelity to the Gospel of Jesus Christ. The mission of the Word in salvation history requires the mission of the Spirit to be effective down through that history. The church through time can only ever be "Christ-centered" if it is "Spirit-led." Only the Spirit can help us to interpret with fidelity the meaning of Christ's Gospel for today. The pope loves to quote the injunction found seven times in the last book of the New Testament: "Hear what the Spirit says to the churches" (Rev 2:7, 11, 17, 29; 3:6, 13, 22). And what is the Spirit's instrument of communication? The *sensus fidei*, as *Lumen Gentium* 12

---

ed. (1871; repr. Westminster, MD: Christian Classics, 1968), 445–68, at 445. The text is also reproduced in John Henry Newman, *On Consulting the Faithful in Matters of Doctrine*, ed. John Coulson (New York: Sheed & Ward, 1961), 109.

teaches. Accordingly, as Pope Francis stated in an address to the International Theological Commission, "Synodality is an ecclesial journey that has a soul that is the Holy Spirit. Without the Holy Spirit there is no synodality."[17] One could add: without synodality, the inspiration of the Third Person of the Trinity is being suppressed.

Second, the notion of "living tradition" is key to the notion of a synodal church. Pope Francis, in commemorating the twenty-fifth anniversary of the promulgation of the Catechism as a collection of the doctrines of the church, summarized all the points of *Dei Verbum* we have noted regarding tradition when he said, "Tradition is a living reality and only a partial vision regards the 'deposit of faith' as something static. The word of God cannot be moth-balled like some old blanket in an attempt to keep insects at bay! No. The word of God is a dynamic and living reality that develops and grows because it is aimed at a fulfillment that none can halt."[18]

Third, the development of the apostolic tradition throughout history is not just the concern of the hierarchy; it is the responsibility of the whole church. As the pope says, "A synodal Church is . . . : The faithful people, the college of bishops, the Bishop of Rome: all listening to each other, and all listening to the Holy Spirit."[19]

Finally, at this writing, we are currently in the ecclesial process of preparing for the two sessions of the General Assembly of the Synod on Synodality. From the perspec-

---

[17] The text is in Italian: "La sinodalità è un cammino ecclesiale che ha un'anima che è lo Spirito Santo. Senza lo Spirito Santo non c'è sinodalità," https://press.vatican.va/content/salastampa/it/bollettino/pubblico/2019/11/29/0938/01934.html.

[18] Francis, Address to Participants in the Meeting Promoted by the Pontifical Council for Promoting the New Evangelization, October 11, 2017.

[19] Francis, 50th anniversary of the institution of the Synod of Bishops, 2015.

tive of *Dei Verbum*, it could be said that the synod process is an opportunity to maintain the vibrancy of the apostolic tradition for the twenty-first century. It will do that if it reengages what I have called elsewhere "the apostolic hermeneutic," that dynamic in the early church already of ongoing interpretation of the received Gospel for what the Scripture scholar Raymond Brown called "the churches the apostles left behind."[20] Accordingly, the 2021–2024 synod hopefully will be an event in the ongoing living tradition of the church, seeking to apply the Gospel of Jesus Christ with fidelity for believers in the twenty-first century.

[20] Raymond E. Brown, *The Churches the Apostles Left Behind* (New York: Paulist Press, 1984).

6

Being the Church in the World

Joys and Griefs, Then and Now

Marcus Mescher

As with the Second Vatican Council on the whole, the Pastoral Constitution on the Church in the Modern World, *Gaudium et Spes*, marks a significant shift in the relationship between the church and the world. Pivoting away from a long history of negative views toward secular society, *Gaudium et Spes* articulates this relationship in terms of "solidarity, respect and love for the whole human family, of which it forms part" (GS 3). Adopting the metaphor of a conversation with the world, *Gaudium et Spes* offers a reading of the "signs of the times" so that members of the church and people around the globe can first sharpen their understanding of reality and then collaborate in the promotion of human dignity and the pursuit of justice and peace (see GS 4). Reflecting Jesus's habit of invitation and inspiration (as opposed to denunciation or coercion), the document provides a rousing encouragement to commit oneself in service to a graced and wounded world. This essay addresses some of the central aspirations of the document, its influence over the last six decades, and how it remains a relevant resource for being a prophetic and pastoral church today.

Elizabeth Johnson recounts what it was like to read an initial draft of *Gaudium et Spes* just before taking her final vows. Poring over the paragraphs, she recalls "drinking it in like water in the desert," moved by this "theological vision of humanity created in the image of God, defaced by the evil of sin, but redeemed by Christ and now led in history by the Spirit through the witness of the church. This was a vision I had never before encountered, and it was so beautiful." By the time she finished reading *Gaudium et Spes*, she concluded, "I was possessed with an overriding conviction: This is worth my life. And so it has proved to be."[1] Reading this document today—especially in the face of rampant religious disaffiliation, upheavals to parish life, and scandals caused by spiritual and sexual abuse—these words sound a call to fidelity not just to Christ or the church, but the whole human family. This spirit of faithfulness is expressed by its memorable opening lines: "The joys and the hopes, the grief and anguish of the people of our time, especially of those who are poor or afflicted, are the joys and hopes, the grief and anguish of the followers of Christ as well. Nothing that is genuinely human fails to find an echo in their hearts" (GS 1). To be part of the Catholic community is to be a person oriented toward encountering others and accompanying them with humility, curiosity, and compassion, forging partnership to create a more humane social order that celebrates unity-in-diversity.

Original Aspirations

Although it is the final document of Vatican II, it would be a grave mistake to consider *Gaudium et Spes* an after-

[1] Elizabeth A. Johnson, "Worth a Life—A Vatican II Story," in *Vatican II: Fifty Personal Stories*, ed. William Madges and Michael J. Daley (Maryknoll, NY: Orbis Books, 2012), 236–40, at 238–39.

thought or addendum. Promulgated on December 7, 1965, by Pope Paul VI, it is a tribute to the spirit of Pope John XXIII, who called the council and urged the bishops to adopt the *ressourcement* and *aggiornamento* that invigorated years of discernment, dialogue, and even debate about what it means to be church *ad intra* and *ad extra*. *Gaudium et Spes* presents a vision of the church *in* the modern world, as distinct from being the church *to* the world (*Ad Gentes*) or *for* the world (*Lumen Gentium*), which is a shocking reversal from countless previous pronouncements written in a tone ranging from condescension to hostility against the world. However, *Gaudium et Spes* remains careful to distinguish itself as in the world but not reducible to it, a unique mixture of sacred and secular, a tertium quid that is both *ecclesia docens* and *ecclesia discens* (GS 39).[2] Calling the church a "third thing" is less about setting it apart than envisioning the church as a dynamic, integrating force in serving the human vocation (a word appearing sixteen times): right-relationship with God and one another. *Gaudium et Spes* articulates a vision of being church where its mission and communion orbit around solidarity with and salvation for everyone (GS 57).

The driving argument of *Gaudium et Spes* is that the church takes responsibility for the world—in faith, hope, and love—to honor the goodness of creation as a partner in the Holy Spirit's redemptive work unfolding in the world (GS 15). This posture is informed by the document's historical context, a moment in time caught between those still reeling from World War II (which claimed the lives of seventy-five million people), feeling a sense of betrayal by the countless Christians who participated in—and even enabled—the rise of fascism and Nazism, shocked by the

[2] Michael J. Himes, "The Church and the World in Conversation: The City of God and 'Interurban' Dialogue," *New Theology Review* 18, no.1 (February 2005): 27–35, at 29–32.

barbarism unleashed by the evil of war, as well as the growing sense of distrust and dread over the spread of communism and the specter of nuclear escalation. *Gaudium et Spes* rejects an Augustinian battle between the City of God and the City of Man; it is not just the "heart of the Council," but as Yves Congar describes, its "promised land."[3] It is worth recalling that a month before the Second Vatican Council began, Pope John XXIII dedicated a radio address on September 11, 1962, to the church that "wishes to be the Church of all, and especially the Church of the poor."[4] The sine qua non is to include the poor in everything the church is and does—to revere and serve Christ who is revealed in the least of our sisters and brothers, as Jesus instructs his disciples (Matt 25:40). Archbishop Dom Hélder Câmara of Brazil likely had this in mind when he interjected, "Are we to spend our whole time discussing internal Church problems while two-thirds of mankind is dying of hunger? What have we to say on the problem of underdevelopment? Will the Council express its concern about the great problems of mankind?"[5] Câmara's probing questions to his brother bishops help shift the image of the pilgrim church in *Lumen Gentium* to a prophetic church in *Gaudium et Spes*.

Although the word "compassion" never appears in the document, a central objective is to speak to and from the

---

[3] Massimo Faggioli, "Vatican II at 50," October 1, 2012, Liguorian, https://www.liguorian.org/vatican-ii-at-50/.

[4] Pope John XXIII, Radio Address concerning the Second Vatican Council, September 11, 1962, https://www.ewtn.com/catholicism/library/radio-address-concerning-the-second-vatican-council-7925; Yves Congar, *Le Concile au jour le jour—Deuxième session* (Paris: Les Éditions du Cerf, 1964).

[5] See Charles Moeller, "Pastoral Constitution on the Church in the Modern World: History of the Constitution," in *Commentary on the Documents of Vatican II*, vol. 5, ed. Herbert Vorgrimler (New York: Herder & Herder, 1969), 1–77, at 10–11.

experience of suffering in showing that the church is attentive to the experience of evil that threatens the dignity and unity of the human family. It echoes Pauline language about the church as a body with many members. Paul observes that if one part suffers, all parts suffer with it, just as if one part is honored, all share in its joy (1 Cor 12:26). A body is not just corporeal, it is porous, susceptible to influence by its surrounding social context. Writing at about this same time, Thomas Merton describes the church as a "Body of broken bones," as "Christ suffers dismemberment" through hatred, violence, and injustice.[6] *Gaudium et Spes* contemplates the wounds marking the Body of Christ due to "vanity and malice" and the "powers of evil" that lead humanity astray (GS 37). These reasons for grief and anxiety ought to inspire all members of the church to be agents of healing by relying on God's endless gifts of grace and love (GS 40). Importantly, this healing work has to move from the interpersonal plane to the political sphere in order to promote human flourishing (GS 75).

Gaudium et Spes's emphasis on the integration of the whole person with all people is a defining trait of this document, the first to address the whole human community. The council fathers explain, "The church is not motivated by earthly ambition but is interested in one thing only—to carry on the work of Christ under the guidance of the Holy Spirit, who came into the world to bear witness to the truth, to save and not to judge, to serve and not to be served" (GS 3). To accomplish this task, the church pledges to read the "signs of the times" and to serve as a social critic, not to condemn the world but to construct a more charitable way of interacting: to "guide each other by sincere dialogue in a spirit of mutual charity and with a genuine concern for the

[6] Thomas Merton, *New Seeds of Contemplation* (New York: New Directions, 1962), 70–79, at 71–72.

common good above all" (GS 43). Although the document itself has been criticized for being overly irenic and idealistic, at its core, it invites readers to see the world as God sees it: with love. Globalizing love broadens horizons for the church to realize "an undreamed-of possibility for love."[7]

Contemplation in love ought to lead to putting love into action. The church in the modern world must be a witness to the dignity of the human person and the sanctity of life in all forms. This means reverencing the "sacrament of our Neighbor" and making a steadfast commitment to advance a more dignified, equitable, and inclusive global community.[8] This is less a matter of "social progress" than the criterion for following Jesus's radical table fellowship, upending social and religious customs by defying dietary restrictions isolating Jews from Gentiles, breaking bread with sinners and outcasts, the oppressed and despised (GS 32). The document does more than propose religious and moral obligations for discipleship; it also advances a robust theological anthropology that honors human dignity and agency as persons-in-community destined to communion with God (GS 19, 24, 32). It stands in stark contrast to a prominent Niebuhrian moral anthropology motivated by insecurity and self-interest where humans inevitably fall prey to sinful desires and group egotism. Instead, *Gaudium et Spes* paints a picture of being human as a vocation to be present to and partner with God who is always and everywhere present, beckoning us to become "the artisans of a new humanity" (GS 30) even as humans are "prone to evil" (GS 25). As the document explains, "Coming to topics which are practical and of some urgency, the council lays stress on respect for

[7] Juan Luis Segundo, *The Community Called Church*, trans. John Drury (Maryknoll, NY: Orbis Books, 1973), 83.

[8] Yves Congar, *The Wide World My Parish: Salvation and Its Problems*, trans. Donald Attwater (Baltimore: Helicon, 1961), 124.

the human person: everybody should look upon his or her neighbor (without any exception) as another self" (GS 27). No person—and therefore, no set of joys and hopes, griefs and anxieties—lies outside one's moral concern.

While universal concern is an aspiration of the Christian moral life, we predictably and sometimes unapologetically fall short. *Gaudium et Spes* suggests this is due to one of the gravest errors of our age: "the dichotomy between the faith which many profess and their day-to-day conduct" (GS 43). This point is made with direct reference to the fulfillment of "responsibilities according to each one's vocation" by those who "immerse [them]selves in earthly activities as if these latter were utterly foreign to religion." The document presents a reciprocal relationship between what the church offers to and receives from the world (GS 40, 44), and when faith is compartmentalized from social responsibility, it undermines the *shalom* that characterizes the unfolding reign of God (GS 39, 40, 57). *Gaudium et Spes* recognizes that the church is not alone in bringing together faith and justice; families are the building blocks of both church and society. In the face of so many urgent social, political, and economic problems, the family is home to the beliefs and practices that honor human dignity, deliver on human rights, and establish vibrant cultural life for all (GS 47, 53). This includes protecting the rights of workers, the dignity of labor, and advancing economic justice in light of the fact that "immense economic inequalities . . . increase daily" (GS 66). These prophetic paragraphs will later inspire the US Catholic Bishops' 1986 pastoral letter, "Economic Justice for All." In words that seem to foreshadow many hallmarks of the papacy of Pope Francis, *Gaudium et Spes* calls on the human community to foster peace, respect differences, invest in dialogue, and forge friendships in celebration of diversity across differences of race and ethnicity, religion, and nationality (GS 92).

Six Decades of Influence

The momentous legacy of *Gaudium et Spes* includes the paradigm shift in Catholic moral theology spurred by the document's discussion of moral conscience. Conscience is not only the place to learn the "natural law" that is "written in their hearts" (Rom 2:15), but it is the "most secret core and . . . sanctuary" of the human person to be "alone with God" (GS 16). Conscience reveals truth, identifies moral norms, and guides a person not only to answer moral questions but to grow in love for what is right, true, good, and just. Etymologically, "conscience" means "to know together," indicating that conscience is a profoundly human process—cutting across religious belief or other differences—of being formed, informed, and transformed. In other words, conscience is not just an inviolable sanctuary for ethical judgment, but a "core relational modality of the human person."[9] Interestingly, *Gaudium et Spes* dedicates much more space to confront the problem of atheism than the few sentences allocated to acknowledge the church's failures to be a credible moral authority due to the "discrepancy between the message it proclaims and the human weakness of those to whom the Gospel has been entrusted" (GS 43). What is more, while *Gaudium et Spes* touts the role of the church as a worldwide authority in conscience formation, it fails to account for how it reconciles differences across various worldviews or solves persistent problems like ignorance, indifference, or inaction that stall collaborative action for justice. As Lisa Cahill contends, "Despite the transformationist agenda of Vatican II and of Catholic social teaching

---

[9] James T. Bretzke, "Moral Theology and the Paradigm Shift of Vatican II," in *The Oxford Handbook of Vatican II*, ed. Catherine E. Clifford and Massimo Faggioli (Oxford: Oxford University Press, 2023), 418–31, at 427.

in general, the evidence of history does not clearly substantiate hope for comprehensive, progressive global change for justice."[10] *Gaudium et Spes* repeatedly celebrates inherent human dignity and the human vocation to freedom and life in communion, but never mentions basic obstacles in the church and world like sexism, racism, heterosexism, ableism, xenophobia, or anti-Semitism. Ignoring these barriers to human dignity, agency, and right-relationships leaves open the question of whether and how we can know—much less do—what is right, true, good, and just together.

Gaudium et Spes makes an important contribution to the canon of Catholic social teaching by serving as a bridge between Pope John XXIII's encyclicals *Mater et Magistra* (1961) and *Pacem in Terris* (1963) and Pope Paul VI's *Populorum Progressio* (1967). But it does so mainly through endorsing progress and development without scrutinizing how global economies rely on unsustainable rates of production and consumption. There is no reference to the patterns of extraction and exploitation that particularly target the Global South or the victimization of Indigenous peoples through colonialism. This represents a missed opportunity to highlight what we might learn from Indigenous beliefs and practices often marked by tremendous reverence for creation and a significantly more harmonious relationship with nature. Instead, *Gaudium et Spes* is filtered through a lens of unashamed anthropocentrism that instrumentalizes all the goods of the earth to human interest, following the claim that humanity is the "center and summit" of creation (GS 12) and "the source, the focus, and the aim of all economic and social life" (GS 63). This myopic ontology betrays what humans owe our covenant partners (God, others, and nonhuman creation, as stated in Genesis 9:9–13),

[10] Lisa Sowle Cahill, "Vatican II, Moral Theology, and Social Ethics," in *The Legacy of Vatican II*, ed. Massimo Faggioli and Andrea Vicini (New York: Paulist Press, 2015), 129–51, at 131.

infecting many church spaces and Christian homes, even after more than three decades of papal statements stressing the "essential" relationship between love of God, neighbor, and nature.[11] In light of widespread climate collapse and sobering numbers of climate refugees displaced from their homes, it remains a troubling legacy that millions of Christians, including many Catholics, do not believe that how we treat creation is a measure for how we love and honor its Creator.

Although *Gaudium et Spes* ignores ecological justice, it plays a vital role in the promotion of social justice as an undeniable springboard for the gathering of the Conference of Latin America Bishops (CELAM) in Medellín, Colombia, in 1968. Here and in subsequent meetings, the bishops of Central and South America practiced reading the "signs of the times" and vigorously championed liberation, solidarity, and the preferential option for the poor. Gustavo Gutiérrez's groundbreaking book, *A Theology of Liberation*, first published in 1971, references *Gaudium et Spes* more than any other church document. Ignacio Ellacuría wrote prolifically that the "signs of the times" are marked by the "crucified people" suffering from poverty, state-sponsored violence, and other violations of human rights. Reading through St. Óscar Romero's pastoral letters, one finds consistent reference to *Gaudium et Spes*, especially its stress on human dignity, the human vocation to forge bonds of loving communion, and the fundamental need to both resist violence and proactively build peace. Insofar as the main metaphor in *Gaudium et Spes* for the relationship between the church and world is a conversation, this is faithfully expressed by

---

[11] See, for example, John Paul II, Message for the World Day of Peace: Peace with God the Creator, Peace with All of Creation, January 1, 1990; Benedict XVI, Message for the World Day of Peace: If You Want to Cultivate Peace, Protect Creation, January 1, 2010; Francis, *Laudato Si'*, May 24, 2015.

Romero's episcopal motto, which read, *Sentir con la iglesia*, translated not simply as "to feel with the church" but "to have one heart and mind with the church." His solidarity with the people of El Salvador, including the seventy-five thousand civilians tortured, disappeared, or killed during its civil war, was an act of deep faith and resolute courage. His prophetic words and actions were inspired by the vision of the church articulated in *Gaudium et Spes*, even as he knew it would cost him his life. It was a price he was willing to pay in order to render credible the church's vow to be a "sign and the safeguard of the transcendental dimension of the human person" (GS 76) that "brings into being the kingdom of God that Jesus promised, and which he continues to proclaim by means of the church's work" for justice and peace.[12] For those who dismiss *Gaudium et Spes* as overly optimistic or even naïve, the blood of martyrs like Ellacuría and Romero provides compelling testimony of the costliness of this eschatological mission to "the body of a new human family . . . foreshadowing in some way the age that is to come" of indivisible unity, justice, and peace (GS 39).

Gaudium et Spes's eschatological hope helped inform the pontificates of John Paul II, Benedict XVI, and Francis. John Paul II referred to *Gaudium et Spes* in every single encyclical he wrote, quoting its influence on the church's witness to universal and innate human dignity, moral freedom and social responsibilities, the dignity of work, the demands of economic justice, and one of his favorite themes: the social holiness expressed through solidarity. Benedict XVI did not engage *Gaudium et Spes* as much, although it gets cited in his 2009 encyclical, *Caritas in Veritate*, connecting love, truth, and integral human development. Even though

[12] Óscar Romero, "The Church's Mission amid the National Crisis," in *Voice of the Voiceless: The Four Pastoral Letters and Other Statements*, trans. Michael J. Walsh (Maryknoll, NY: Orbis Books, 1985), 142.

Benedict XVI was less forceful in connecting Christian faith to working for justice, he was still adamant that salvation history unites spiritual, social, political, economic, and ecological right-relationship across God's wondrous creation. Turning to Francis, it seems difficult to imagine his papacy without *Gaudium et Spes*, especially given his concerted effort to bring people together across differences to build a "culture of encounter." Hallmarks of Francis's pontificate—mercy as the identifier for who God is and what God wants, the importance of discernment and dialogue, and his constant urging to stretch our imagination to create a more open world—all find their roots in *Gaudium et Spes* and its vision of the human person who "cannot live, develop, and find fulfillment except 'in the sincere gift of self to others' " (*Fratelli Tutti*, no. 87, quoting GS 24).[13]

Reading *Gaudium et Spes* Today

If we listen for the "joys and hopes, griefs and anxieties" of the people of this age, what would we hear? We only know when we draw near to one another, especially to those who question if they count, matter, or belong to the communities we inhabit. This requires that the church create the conditions for people to know others and be known by others through cultivating a sense of mutual respect and trust, aiming to repair relationships broken by contempt or condemnation that are all too common especially in social media interactions. Pope Francis's recommitment to synodality frames how to be the church in the modern world in terms of journeying together and listening to one another. However, in light of the fact that millions of Catholics no longer belong to local parishes or attend Mass, it raises existential questions about where the Body of Christ might

---

[13] Francis, *Fratelli Tutti*—Encyclical Letter on Fraternity and Social Friendship, October 3, 2020.

be found. Why have so many people—especially young people—decided that being part of the church is neither purposeful nor generative? It is perhaps related to the church's damaged moral credibility due to the pain caused by failing to welcome, affirm, and empower its members—especially women, people of color, and LGBTQ+ individuals. In too many places, we have witnessed a church more in love with power than witnessing the power of love, calling to mind Henri Nouwen's reflection, "What makes the temptation to power so seemingly irresistible? Maybe it is that power offers an easy substitute for the hard task of love."[14]

Reading *Gaudium et Spes* today raises major questions for what it means to be church *ad intra* and *ad extra*. Today the church enjoys much less status and influence than it did during Vatican II. Perhaps this means that it has less to lose in raising its prophetic voice in defense of human dignity, human rights, and the conditions necessary for personal and collective flourishing. Karl Rahner's observation remains relevant as ever: "The task of the Church as critic of society is still to a large extent neglected and remains unfulfilled. . . . [The Church] is still far from having fulfilled in sufficient measure what she herself declares to be her mission. . . . We have pronounced judgment upon ourselves in saying that the Church is not yet that which the present and the future require her to be."[15] As long as hypocrisy, corruption, and the abuse of power mark the church, it will not be a credible witness to the human vocation of the fullness of life for all that it has long preached.

It is one thing to acknowledge the church as sinful or even as a source of suffering. While it is true that the

[14] Henri J. M. Nouwen, *In the Name of Jesus: Reflections on Christian Leadership* (New York: Crossroad, 1989), 59.

[15] Karl Rahner, "The Function of the Church as Critic of Society," in *Theological Investigations*, vol. 12, trans. David Bourke (New York: Seabury, 1974), 229–49, at 249.

church must bear witness to the crucified Body of Christ, we must never grow numb to the suffering inflicted by the church on its own members. The grave betrayal of sexual abuse by clergy and its concealment by church officials has caused unimaginable harm, spanning psychological distress, spiritual anguish, moral disorientation, social isolation, and institutional distrust. There are no adequate words and actions to express the necessary remorse, repentance, and atonement. The church remains slow in delivering on its promise of transparency, accountability, and prevention, to say nothing of the restorative work with survivors and their loved ones. The global legacy of clergy abuse reflects an idolatrous obsession with power, and while that may not be a new feature of being church, the fact that it persists is a reason for lamentation. We are still a long way from the church heeding the words of Shawn Copeland: "Like Jesus, the church must be willing to risk fortune and future for the sake of those who are abandoned to the scrap heap of history."[16] Reading the "signs of the times" today, there is ample evidence of division and pain in both the church and world, leaving the hard task of love a dauntingly tall order. But revisiting *Gaudium et Spes* and those who were inspired by it—like Merton and Romero—is a reminder to trust in the power of love. Merton contends that the "Body of broken bones" stands in need of "the sacrifice and sorrow that are the price of this resetting of bones."[17] Pope Francis has called for a church that is less like a fortress and more like a field hospital, tending to wounds after battle. But this metaphor is problematic for two reasons: first, the scale of

---

[16] M. Shawn Copeland, "The Church Is Marked by Suffering," in *The Many Marks of the Church*, ed. William Madges and Michael J. Daley (New London, CT: Twenty-Third Publications, 2006), 212–16, at 215.

[17] Merton, *New Seeds of Contemplation*, 72.

harm requires much more than triage; second, if the church is responsible for the wounding, it may not be a safe place for healing the spiritual and social wounds that mark the Body of Christ.

Still, we can find some moving examples of clergy trying to be "shepherds who smell like their sheep," as Pope Francis has pled. Cardinal McElroy in San Diego has advanced synodality around marriage and family life, practicing mercy and inclusion in the pastoral directives of *Amoris Laetitia*,[18] so that the church can better support and empower families trying to find their way toward right relationship. Bishop John Stowe in Lexington, Kentucky, prioritizes the needs of Black Catholics enduring white supremacy, mobilizes pastoral care and charitable assistance to the poorest of the poor in Appalachia, and vociferously calls for peace through his work with Pax Christi and his ministry to the LGBTQ community. But the needs in and beyond the church fall on all our shoulders. *Lumen Gentium* describes the church not just as a sheepfold in need of good shepherds, but as "a choice vineyard" such that we are all coworkers in the vineyard (LG 6). Today the labor is regrettably quite great, and the laborers, even more regrettably, are quite few. The church is growing fastest in the Global South, where people still feel more talked about than heard, included, or empowered. In the United States, Hispanic Catholics are a growing share of the church—and will soon be a majority of its members—but often are overlooked and unrepresented in theology, ministry, and church leadership. For many, the church has been reduced to the place where sacraments get distributed, a vision of the church that reinforces clericalism, hierarchicalism, and consumerism—where the church is a place to go to get something rather than the lifeblood of community or relationships characterized by dignity and

[18] Francis, *Amoris Laetitia*, March 19, 2026.

freedom, mutual respect and concern, as co-responsible artisans of peace and justice.

Gaudium et Spes closes by asserting that "Christians can yearn for nothing more ardently than to serve the people of this age successfully with increasing generosity. Holding loyally to the Gospel, enriched by its resources, and joining forces with all who love and practice justice, they have shouldered a weighty task here on earth" (GS 93). The hard work of love is an enormous and unending task, and I daresay it's even harder in 2023 than it was in 1965. Many of us feel stretched, if not overwhelmed, maybe even just holding on by a thread of grace. Which is why, now more than ever, we can find motivation in the words of *Gaudium et Spes* that remind us that we are constantly recipients of grace, enlivened by the Holy Spirit who sustains and strengthens us by sharing access to the power of God-who-is-Love (1 John 4:8). Love is what is given to us and asked of us, just as the final paragraph of *Gaudium et Spes* articulates, invoking Jesus's line that "by this all will know that you are my disciples, if you have love for one another" (John 13:35). The joys and hopes, griefs and sorrows of the people of this age stem from our successes and failures in the hard work of love. So must these joys and hopes, griefs and sorrows be ours, who are followers of Christ.[19]

[19] The author would like to acknowledge Michael Daley and Martin Madar for their helpful input on this essay.

7

Beyond "Women in the Church"

Gender and Ecclesiology since Vatican II

Elyse J. Raby

The topic of "women in the church" is well-trod ground—even more so, "women in the church since Vatican II." There is no shortage of books and articles describing women's roles in the church, the progress they have made in recent decades, their contributions to spirituality and the daily life of the church, their hopes and visions for the future, and the ongoing need for their full equality, visibility, and participation in the church. At every major anniversary of the Second Vatican Council, one scholar or another has addressed the status of women in the church at that milestone.

This chapter continues in that tradition. In some ways, it simply affirms what has already been said at prior anniversaries of the council. But I also reframe the subject of inquiry in order to see what is new about the story of "women in the church" between the fiftieth and sixtieth anniversaries of the council—a period that roughly coincides with Pope Francis's papacy. Hence the title for this chapter indicates that we will go *beyond* the usual question of "women in the church" to consider how gender and ecclesiology—the field of theology that speaks about the church—have become increasingly intertwined since Vatican II. In spite of (or perhaps because of) the progress made over the last sixty years regarding women's admittance into ministry, academic theology, and curial positions, there has been a simultaneous counterforce developing—a theology of gender complementarity—that limits the full participation of women and the LGBTQ community in the church.

Women at Vatican II

When the first session of Vatican II opened in October 1962, there were no women or lay auditors present. Paul VI invited twelve lay auditors to the second session in 1963, all of them male. In October of that year, the Belgian cardinal Leo Suenens observed that half the church was missing from the council since no women were present; he then called for an increase in the number and diversity of lay auditors. Subsequently, twenty-three women from fifteen different countries were invited to the third and fourth sessions.[1] Of these women, ten were vowed religious; nine were single, never married; three were widowed; and one was married (and her husband was also an auditor).

For many of these women, preparation for the council had begun decades earlier. They had been deeply involved in lay movements or women's associations at national or international levels; some were already well known to their local bishop or to curial offices. The women religious were typically superiors of their respective religious congregations or presidents of national or international organizations of women religious or both. Some of these women had even

[1] Carmel McEnroy's book *Guests in Their Own House: The Women of Vatican II* (New York: Crossroad, 1996) is the first, and definitive, account of the women auditors at Vatican II. I am indebted to her work throughout this chapter.

made efforts to share their expertise with the council before they were named as auditors. For example, Pilar Bellosillo, the Spanish president of the World Union of Catholic Women's Organizations (WUCWO), an international lay movement representing twenty-six million Catholics worldwide, had sent notes to the commissions on topics concerning women, the family, and the lay apostolate even before she was an auditor. Similarly, after being named auditors but before heading to Rome, the married couple Luz-María and José Álvarez-Icaza, members of the Christian Family Movement, visited thirty-six countries to gather input and prepare for the council. They also sent out questionnaires, receiving forty thousand responses, which they shared at the council with bishops, theologians, and religious.

When the women auditors arrived in Rome, Pope Paul VI invited them to attend "sessions of interest to women"—which, as it turned out, was all of them. As Carmel McEnroy notes, "They showed up for everything—Mass, formal conciliar sessions, press briefings, special lectures, social gatherings, as well as their own auditors' meetings."[2] As auditors, they were never permitted to speak on the council floor; however, they were able to speak with bishops and theologians during evening meals and other informal gatherings. Moreover, the moral theologian Bernhard Häring single-handedly made sure that women were invited to the working commissions on the conciliar documents. The women read the documents, discussed them, and gave their input to the commissions. Their impact was most significant on the council's statements on sex discrimination, on women's engagement in the social and cultural world, on the need for lay men and women to study theology, and on married life.

The women auditors also had an important impact on

[2] McEnroy, *Guests in Their Own House*, 120.

what the council documents *did not* say about women. One of the North American auditors, Sr. Mary Luke Tobin, recounted the story of an interaction between the French theologian Yves Congar and Rosemary Goldie, an Australian lay woman well known in Rome for her work with international lay movements. During the commission's work drafting *Gaudium et Spes*, Congar read a flowery paragraph he had written about women, "and to his surprise, there was no response from the women. 'Rosemary,' he said, 'don't you like it?' 'No,' she replied, 'you can cut out all the references to women as flowers and light, etc. We don't need any of that grandiose stuff that has no basis in women's reality. All we want is to be treated as full human beings, accorded the same equality as men.' "[3] Bellosillo made the same point to bishops, saying "this kind of language is detached from life [and] puts women on a pedestal instead of on the same level as man. By doing so, you demonstrate that in reality you consider *man* the human being, but not woman."[4] Catherine Clifford observes that, rather than giving their approval to texts on women's apostolic work as distinct from men's, "the women at Vatican II understood themselves to be included fully each time the council referred to the members of the baptized faithful."[5] Thus, everything the council said about the people of God, the dignity and equality of baptism, the common priesthood, the lay apostolate, and so on—all of this pertains to women just as it does to men. In the eyes of the conciliar women, any further definition of women's

[3] McEnroy, *Guests in Their Own House,* 109. See also Mary Luke Tobin, "Women in the Church: Vatican II and After," *Ecumenical Review* 37 (1985): 295–305, at 296, where she recounts the full story.

[4] McEnroy, *Guests in Their Own House,* 139 (emphasis in original).

[5] Catherine E. Clifford, *Decoding Vatican II: Interpretation and Ongoing Reception* (New York: Paulist Press, 2014), 73.

dignity or roles in the church would limit them and isolate them to a dehumanizing pedestal.

Women in the Council Documents

The texts of Vatican II mention women specifically in at least thirty-eight articles across ten of the sixteen conciliar documents. There are about nineteen references to women in general, sixteen references to women religious, and seven references to women specifically as mothers and wives. In the majority of these references, the texts speak of men and women as equally constituting and contributing to humanity. Women are seen as social, moral, and intellectual agents who share in Christ's role as priest, prophet, and king. For example, the texts state that women, like men, provide for themselves, their families, and society; they are "authors and artisans of culture"; promoters of ecumenical dialogue; catechists and missionaries, educators in Catholic schools and witnesses to the Gospel in their public, social, and professional lives (GS 55; AA 14; AG 17, 21; GE conclusion). The texts also affirm the movement for women's equality as a positive development in the world, and *Gaudium et Spes* rejects "any kind of social or cultural discrimination in basic personal rights on the grounds of sex, race, color, social conditions," and so on as "incompatible with God's design" (GS 29).

When women are spoken of in their roles as wives and mothers, this is not set in contrast to their social progress (GS 52). The section on marriage in *Gaudium et Spes* speaks of the dignity of both motherhood *and* fatherhood, and of the duty of *both* parents to devote themselves to their children's education. The social context of marriage and family life is also acknowledged, and the council calls for the economy and workforce to be adjusted to the needs of the person, "with special attention to domestic life, that of mothers of families in particular" (GS 67). Overall, the council recognizes and affirms women's maternal and domestic contributions, while also supporting women's social progress and fundamental human rights.

Once again, it is crucial to notice what the council documents *do not* say. There is no description of who or what women are, what their distinctive nature is, or what their proper role is in the church (beyond what is proper to the laity). They are not reduced to maternal or spousal identities, and are not described as complements to men. Women's contributions to the church are also not spoken of in stereotyped ways—they are not described as having any particular charisms due to their sensitivity, nurturing capacities, their likeness to Mary, or anything of the sort. They are generally described simply as capable humans and members of the lay faithful—and we have the women auditors to thank for that.

After the Council

In the decades following the council, women's participation in the life and ministry of the church expanded in ways hardly dreamed of by the council itself. Lay ministry exploded after the council, to the point that there are currently some thirty thousand women working in ministry in the United States. Along with this, women pursued graduate degrees in theology and ministry in increasing numbers. We are now in the third generation of women theologians entering the academy. Communities of women religious undertook the in-depth and sometimes painful process of renewal called for by Vatican II and "began to move beyond the traditional apostolates of nursing and teaching to embrace peace and social justice ministries."[6]

[6] Mary Ann Hinsdale, "A Feminist Reflection on Postconciliar Catholic Ecclesiology," in *A Church with Open Doors: Catholic*

The call for women's ordination to the priesthood is, of course, another significant postconciliar development. This movement began before the council (women's groups even advocated for discussion of the issue at the council), but it gained much more momentum afterward, since the council was experienced as a moment of new hope and openness in the church, and the texts condemned any discrimination on account of sex (see GS 29). The Vatican issued a clear "no" to women's priestly ordination under Paul VI in 1976 and again under John Paul II in 1994, but this did not shut down the conversation. Women have continued seeking full baptismal equality in the Catholic Church through avenues such as the Women-Church movement, Roman Catholic Women Priests, Women's Ordination Conference, and Future Church. Of course, some have simply left altogether, pursuing ministry and leadership in other churches or on the ecclesial margins.

More recently, Pope Francis has opened new doors, new offices, and new conversations about women's participation in the ministry and governance of the church. He has appointed (a record-breaking) nine women to the International Theological Commission in the first decade of his pontificate. He formally opened to women the instituted ministries of lector and acolyte (created by Paul VI in 1973 for men), and he created the new instituted ministry of catechist, also open to both women and men. He has appointed five women to key leadership positions in the Vatican, including to the dicastery that advises on the selection of bishops. Although only one of these positions is held by a nonreligious woman thus far, their appointments are symbolically and canonically significant. With Sr. Nathalie Becquart's appointment as undersecretary to the Synod of Bishops in

---

Ecclesiology for the Third Millennium, ed. Richard R. Gaillardetz and Edward P. Hahnenberg (Collegeville, MN: Liturgical Press, 2015), 112–37, at 117–18.

2021, it became possible, for the first time in the church's history, for a woman to vote in the Synod of Bishops. With Francis's reforms of the Roman Curia in 2022, it became possible for a woman to head a Vatican dicastery as well. Finally, Francis also created two commissions to study the restoration of women to the diaconate.

In many ways, then, women have undoubtedly advanced in the church since Vatican II. Women were hardly thought of prior to, and in the first years of, the council; sixty years later, women can head a Vatican dicastery. And yet there are many ways in which women have not advanced in equality since Vatican II—not just in terms of the limits on their sacramental ministry, but in terms of what "woman" symbolizes in magisterial texts and how gender functions in the church. For at the very same time that women were pursuing theology degrees, reforming religious life, and entering professional ministry, a theology was developing that would undermine, or at least put a limit on, all of this. It is at this point that I want to shift from a conversation about "women's roles in the church" to a broader consideration of how gender functions in Catholic theology.

Complementarity: A Postconciliar Development

As noted above, the women auditors at the council resisted "the flowery adjectives, the pedestals and incense" about women in the draft documents; they insisted that women be seen as *human*—nothing more, nothing less.[7] Moreover, Vatican II did not define women's nature or describe them as having any particular gifts simply by virtue of being women. This began to change under Pope John Paul II, whose "theology of the body" has become the normative

[7] Tobin, "Women in the Church," 296, quoting Rosemary Goldie.

theological perspective of the magisterium regarding sex, gender, and sexuality.[8]

At the heart of John Paul II's theology of the body are two ideas—gender essentialism and gender complementarity. John Paul II held that one's sexual identity as male and female is given by God as a gift and is an essential, foundational aspect of the human person. Anatomical sex determines the psychological, affective, social, and spiritual elements of a person. Moreover, male and female are complementary, two "modes" of human nature, each made for the other; this is the basis of the family in God's plan of creation. They complement one another not just sexually but spiritually and psychologically as well, in both family life and in the public sphere. The late pope saw the two creation accounts in Genesis as revealing these truths. The fact that male and female are made together in God's image in Genesis 1 means they are made for union with one another; the story in Genesis 2 of Eve made from Adam's side indicates that women complement men and they fulfill one another in marriage.

In the development of this theology, the nature of "woman" has received detailed theological description—precisely the kind of description that the conciliar women resisted. Both John Paul II and Joseph Ratzinger taught that a woman's nature is fundamentally marked by her capacity to bear a child.[9] Because of the structure and role of female reproductive organs, women have a distinct "capacity for

---

[8] John Paul II began this work as a private theologian in the 1960s and continued to develop it throughout his Wednesday audiences as pope in the late '70s through the '90s, as well as in *Mulieris Dignitatem*, his 1988 Apostolic Letter On the Dignity and Vocation of Women, and his Letter to Women, June 29, 1995.

[9] Joseph Ratzinger, as head of the Congregation for the Doctrine of the Faith under John Paul II, issued a "Letter on the Collaboration of Men and Women in the Church and in the World," May 31, 2004.

the other" and "readiness to accept life," and therefore are naturally intuitive, generous, receptive, sensitive, and faithful.[10] (This is often called the "feminine genius.") Women's vocation is thus fulfilled in motherhood—either biological or spiritual, in the case of vowed virginity. Mary, Mother of God, is the archetype of womanhood.

John Paul II develops this theology of complementarity primarily in relation to marriage and women's roles in the family and society, but he also extends it to the church more broadly. Heterosexual marriage is a key metaphor for the church in his thought—Christ the (male) Bridegroom unites himself to the (feminine) Church, his bride. This is expressed sacramentally in the Eucharist, in which Christ gives his body and pours out his blood, "creating" the church and uniting himself to her. This is one reason why, for John Paul II, women are excluded from the priesthood—not only must the priest bear a natural resemblance to Christ, the male partner of the female church, but the eucharistic act of giving of one's body and blood is (somehow) a masculine act.[11]

In short, John Paul II's theology of women and sex/gender, which is derived from his theology of marriage, is then projected onto the church writ large and its ministry. The very nature of the church is described as a male-female union; salvation itself comes through this male-female union. This is why Mary Ann Hinsdale rightly calls complementarity "*the* issue under the issues in ecclesiology today."[12]

There are two valuable components of this anthropology. First, it retains the important truth that humans are innately

---

[10] Ratzinger, "On the Collaboration of Men and Women," no. 13; John Paul II, *Mulieris Dignitatem,* nos. 14, 18; John Paul II, Letter to Women, nos. 2–3.

[11] John Paul II, *Mulieris Dignitatem*, no. 26.

[12] Hinsdale, "A Feminist Reflection," 118.

social beings. Likewise, it takes seriously the body in all its dimensions, and therefore is a properly incarnational theology. Many theologians, however, female and male alike, have critiqued gender complementarity over the past few decades for several reasons. Two of these critiques stand out. First, this theology of complementarity understands the sexed body primarily through a selective reading of Scripture passages and ecclesial symbols (often interpreted through medieval understandings of reproduction), forgoing attention to lived experience or contemporary natural sciences, which do *not* always reveal a rigid sexual binary. Second, it boxes women into cultural stereotypes and retains a gendered hierarchy in church and society *even as* it asserts equality between women and men. In this way, complementarity is often a justification for reigning patriarchal structures in the church. (It is also worth noting that there is no papal document "on the dignity and vocation of men," perhaps because "man" is seen as the normative, default mode of being human; woman is the "other" whose existence calls for a special theology.)

Nevertheless, Pope Francis has also espoused gender essentialism and complementarity and has a lofty, sentimentalized view of women. For example, he has said that "women are the most beautiful thing God has made,"[13] and somewhat infamously referred to the women on the International Theological Commission as "strawberries on the cake"[14] who "think differently from men and make theology something deeper and also more 'flavorful.'"[15]

---

[13] Interview with Franca Giansoldati, *Aleteia*, June 30, 2014, quoted in Hinsdale, "A Feminist Reflection," 119–20.

[14] Hannah Roberts, "Women Theologians are 'the Strawberry on the Cake,' Says Pope," *The Tablet*, December 11, 2014.

[15] Rome Reports, "Pope Francis: Increase Number of Women in Commission as They Add 'Flavor' to Theology," November 24, 2022.

In his 2013 encyclical *Evangelii Gaudium*, Pope Francis argued that women should have a greater presence in the church and in society because of "the sensitivity, intuition, and other distinctive skill sets which they, more than men, tend to possess."[16] In other words, women should be allowed a seat at the metaphorical table *not* because of their leadership skills, theological acumen, or professional expertise, but because they are seen as innately sensitive and oriented toward others—mainly, recall, because they have the capacity for childbirth. Pope Francis not only echoes the thought of John Paul II and Benedict in these matters, but also takes it a step further, in two ways: first, in how he extends women's "Marian identity" throughout ecclesial ministry more broadly, and second, in how complementarity has developed into a battle against so-called gender ideology during his papacy.

In his encyclical *Querida Amazonia,* rather than reopening the diaconate to women at that time, Francis called the church "to encourage the emergence of other forms of service *and charisms* that are proper to women" and "in a way that reflects their womanhood."[17] He says that priests must be male because the priest is an icon of Christ, a male; women are, instead icons of Mary.[18] As such, women have "simple and straightforward" gifts to offer the church. Francis does encourage the creation of recognized, public ministries for women, but only those "that do not entail Holy Orders and that can better signify the role that is theirs," which is to "[make] present the tender strength of Mary, the Mother."[19] He developed this further and con-

---

[16] Francis, *Evangelii Gaudium*, November 24, 2013, no. 103.

[17] Francis, *Querida Amazonia,* February 2, 2020, nos. 102–3 (emphasis added).

[18] Francis, *Querida Amazonia,* no. 101.

[19] Francis, *Querida Amazonia,* nos. 103 and 101.

tinued to place women on a pedestal in a November 2022 interview. He affirmed that there should be more room for women in the administrative dimension of the church, but the Petrine, ministerial principle of the church "has no place" for them. "One has to be in the Marian principle, which is more important. Woman is more, she looks more like the church, which is mother and spouse."[20]

In other words, for Francis, gender is a determining factor not just for ecclesial office, priestly ministry, and sacramental function (as was the case with John Paul II and Benedict XVI), but also for charism. In this view, charisms—those gifts of the Holy Spirit to the individual for the sake of building up the church—are determined by one's biological sex. And sex is so significant for the church that only men can properly symbolize Christ or Peter; women can only symbolize Mary. In an ecclesiology of complementarity, women remain caretakers and support staff, not leaders.

Second, gender essentialism and complementarity have become even more entrenched recently through the increased condemnations of "gender ideology" by Pope Francis, documents from the Vatican, and diocesan policies. The phrase "gender ideology" is often used to refer to the philosophical, scientific, and/or cultural views that sex is nonbinary (i.e., there is more than male and female) and/or that sex and gender are potentially unrelated, and to some extent subjective categories (e.g., one can be assigned male at birth but later identify as a woman). The phrase "gender ideology" is also aimed at those who identify and live publicly as queer, trans, or nonbinary (i.e., those who feel that the sex assigned to them at birth does not cohere with their sense of self or the social expectations

[20] Interview with *America*, November 22, 2022, https://www.americamagazine.org/faith/2022/11/28/pope-francis-interview-america-244225.

placed on them) and at any public policies that promote or protect these ideas.

In 2019, the Vatican's Congregation for Catholic Education (CCE) issued "Male and Female He Created Them," the first document from the Vatican to focus specifically on "gender ideology." It was not issued by Pope Francis himself, but it frequently cites his encyclicals *Amoris Laetitia* and *Laudato Si'* as well as several documents by John Paul II and Benedict XVI. The document sees gender ideology as denying the differences between men and women that lie at the heart of the human person and the family. It also sees "gender ideology" and "transgenderism" as a kind of hyperindividualism and a dualism that absolutizes subjective feelings and reduces the body to "inert matter."[21] In short, the CCE unequivocally rejects public or educational policies that encourage the social acceptance of queer, trans, or nonbinary identities and calls for Catholic schools and formators to teach clearly the truth of human sexuality as developed by John Paul II and his successors. The CCE document has been a springboard for bishops in the United States and around the world to craft anti-trans policies for their dioceses, parishes, and schools. In recent years, dozens of dioceses in the United States alone have issued policies requiring that students be treated only according to the sex indicated on their birth certificate, prohibiting the use of "chosen names/pronouns" or other forms of social acceptance of transgender identities, and encouraging parents of children with gender dysphoria to seek pastoral care and avoid any medical or psychological care that is incompatible with Catholic teaching.

A full engagement with gender theory and dialogue with

---

[21] Congregation for Catholic Education, "'Male and Female He Created Them': Towards a Path of Dialogue on the Question of Gender Theory in Education," Vatican City, 2019, no. 20.

the lives of LGBTQ individuals is well beyond the scope of this essay. I simply point out here how this increased condemnation of "gender ideology" relates to our broader topic of women in the church since Vatican II. Since the council, we have seen a steady increase in the centrality of male-female sex difference to the whole of Catholic ecclesiology. Gender essentialism and complementarity began as a theology of "woman," itself rooted in a theology of heterosexual marriage, to explain women's dignity and distinctive gifts. But it has evolved to *also* express distinctions in ministry, the symbolic function of the priesthood, the mystery of the Eucharist, and indeed, the mystery of our salvation in Christ. Because gender complementarity functions so broadly now, nonbinary sex/gender identities, and the very notion of gender identity as distinct from biology, are seen as undermining the entire ecclesial, sacramental, and symbolic order. This is why I suggest that gender, and the relationship between gender and ecclesiology, is more fundamental and significant today than simply asking about "women's roles" in the church. Women—at least cisgender, heterosexual women—are no longer (and maybe never were) *the* marginalized, overlooked demographic in the church, and "gender" in papal documents is no longer just about women but about anyone whose lives or bodies challenge the male-female binary articulated so strongly in the past fifty years.

The Road Ahead

In 1985, Sr. Mary Luke Tobin noted that the "depersonalization of women through humor, ridicule, or simply metaphor" continued to alienate women in the church and society, even twenty years after the council. At the fiftieth anniversary of the council, Susan Ross wrote that in spite of the progress for women in the church since the council, "the official Roman Catholic theology of womanhood has remained remarkably unchanged. It has been developed into a theology of complementarity . . . [that] sees women primarily as mothers and partners who respond to the leadership and initiative of God and men."[22] I have suggested that the situation is much the same, perhaps even a bit worse, sixty years out from the council. Is there a way out of this impasse? What is needed for a fuller affirmation of the dignity of women and LGBTQ Catholics and deeper integration of their varied gifts into the life of the church?

First, I would argue that we do *not* need "a theology of the woman," as Pope Francis suggests.[23] Such a theology would most likely reinscribe women as "the other," as having a "special nature," as symbols rather than subjects. Exaltation is not equality. Vatican II's silence on "women's nature" and avoidance of stereotyping and overdefining women is well worth retrieving in this regard. A "theology of women" would also undoubtedly reinforce gender complementarity, which leaves no room for LGBTQ Catholics in the church. Instead, we should strive for an understanding of gender and human sexuality more broadly—one that is not simply a theology of heterosexual marriage, but instead listens deeply to the lives of women (queer women, trans women, and gay/lesbian women included) and trans men, queer men, and nonbinary people, and thoroughly engages contemporary human and natural sciences, not simply Scripture and tradition.[24] We might also follow in

---

[22] Susan A. Ross, "Joys and Hopes, Griefs and Anxieties: Catholic Women since Vatican II," *New Theology Review* 25 (March 2013): 37.

[23] Francis, "A Big Heart Open to God," interview by Antonio Spadaro, September 30, 2013, https://www.vatican.va/content/francesco/en/speeches/2013/september/documents/papa-francesco_20130921_intervista-spadaro.html.

[24] Much of this work is already being done, for example, by theo-

the pattern of the conciliar women who insisted that any talk about "the baptized faithful" included them. In our day, any talk about the laity and their contributions to and participation in the church can, and must, be understood as including LGBTQ Catholics.

Second, ecclesiology needs to resist the growing link between gender and charism. In 1 Corinthians, where we hear about the many different gifts and manifestations of the Spirit, there is no indication whatsoever that these gifts or charisms are given on the basis of sex/gender or as reflections of one's proper gender role in the church. Quite the opposite—St. Paul says, "One and the same Spirit produces all of these, distributing them individually to each person as he wishes" (1 Cor 12:11). Women have the gifts of the Spirit not because of their reproductive anatomy but because they are people, baptized in Christ. Likewise, LGBTQ Catholics have gifts of the Spirit because they are people, baptized in Christ. So long as gender complementarity and essentialism remain the framework for understanding the human person, charism, ministerial responsibility, and the church's relationship with Christ, the individual women who hold positions of governance will remain the exception to the norm, rather than a sign of the freedom in which the Spirit gifts the church and the truth that women, and all people, are called to be icons of Christ.

I have hope that these visions might become reality. This hope comes from the women at Vatican II, and our own "conciliar women," or rather "synodal women," today. Recall that the women auditors at Vatican II were deeply active in the church well before Vatican II. They were not chosen as auditors out of nowhere; they were chosen for their recognized expertise and leadership of national and

---

logians Patrick Cheng, Susannah Cornwall, Craig Ford Jr., Justin Sabia-Tanis, Paul Schutz, Linn Tonstad, and others.

international lay organizations and religious communities. The church—the people of God and communities of the faithful—recognized them as leaders, supported their work, and acknowledged their authority long before they were brought into any "official" capacity by Rome. These brilliant, experienced, organized women then made sure that conciliar texts recognize *all* women as fully human and as active agents in the life of the church. The women involved in the 2021–2024 Synod on Synodality have similar stories. They were already leading theologians, organizers, or women religious; they had already been involved in prior synods; their authority and gifts were already acknowledged by their local communities before being recognized and lifted up by Rome.[25] They and countless other women have long been doing the work that will bear fruit in this or the next synod, or at some future council. We can hope that if we continue to cultivate, support, and recognize women's leadership, authority, and ministry in the present, this will eventually be given formal and public recognition in the future.

A point of difference between the council and the Synod on Synodality is reason for hope as well. Women were an afterthought at Vatican II; they were brought in only at the third and fourth sessions, and so their only impact on texts were on *Gaudium et Spes* and *Apostolicam Actuositatem*, which were still in draft form in the later sessions. In the Synod on Synodality, however, women have been active and present from the beginning, in listening sessions, in coordinating meetings, and in the drafting of documents—as,

[25] For example, Sr. Nathalie Becquart, undersecretary of the Synod of Bishops, was a coordinator, speaker, and observer at the 2018 synod on young people and a consultor to the General Secretariat for the 2019 synod on the Amazon. Dr. Kristin Colberg, a member of the synod's theological commission, is associate professor of theology at St. John's School of Theology in Collegeville, MN.

to some extent, have LGBTQ Catholics. Their impact can be seen in reports from various stages of the synod. For example, the document of the Continental Stage makes several mentions of the equal dignity, co-responsibility, and mission of all the baptized, women and men alike.[26] It reflects a desire for a more welcoming, inclusive church—one that dialogues with those on the peripheries (which include LGBTQ people and women). It acknowledges that all over the world, on all continents, and in almost all reports, the church called "for Catholic women to be valued first and foremost as baptized and equal members of the People of God" whose contributions and charisms are valued and who have full and equal participation in the life of the church.[27] It also notes that many reports asked the church to continue discerning the active role of women in church governance, the possibility of allowing women to preach in parishes, and readmitting women to the diaconate. In short, the synod has heard women's voices: "It is clear that the Church must find ways . . . to enable women to participate more fully at all levels of Church life."[28]

Vatican II was not perfect, and it was not an end point. The bishops at Vatican II certainly did not envision the explosion of women in ministry that is part of our reality today, and the women auditors themselves may not have imagined this either. But here we are. The Synod on Synodality is not perfect either, but it too is not an end point. In this synodal process, we too may be setting down stepping-stones toward a future we cannot yet imagine, just as Vatican II did. Constantina Baldinucci, an auditor at Vatican II, summed up the council, saying, "A world is

---

[26] General Secretariat of the Synod, "Enlarge the Space of Your Tent: Working Document for the Continental Stage," Vatican City, October 2022, nos. 11.3, 22, 57, 60–65, 66.

[27] "Enlarge the Space of Your Tent," no. 61.

[28] "Enlarge the Space of Your Tent," no. 61.

dying, and a new one is being created with the wealth of contributions of interest to all people. Nothing higher or more majestic could be thought of on this earth about this assembly in which the protagonist is the Holy Spirit itself."[29]

[29] McEnroy, *Guests in Their Own House*, 98.

8

Nostra Aetate

Journey to Interfaith Dialogue

Celia Deutsch, NDS

Nostra Aetate is one of the shortest documents promulgated by the Second Vatican Council. It was also one of the most controversial. In this brief essay, I would like to reflect on the content, reception, and continuing relevance of that text.[1] I reflect briefly on current challenges in relation to ongoing reception of the document, particularly in the context of the United States.

---

[1] For accounts of the history of the writing and promulgation of *Nostra Aetate*, especially paragraph 4, see John M. Oesterreicher, "Declaration of the Relationship of the Church to Non-Christian Religions," in *Commentary on the Documents of Vatican*, vol. 3, ed. Herbert Vorgrimler, trans. William Glen-Doepel et al. (London: Burns and Oates, 1969), 3:1–136; Giovanni Miccoli, "Two Sensitive Issues: Religious Freedom and the Jews," in *History of Vatican II*, 5 vols., ed. Giuseppe Alberigo and Joseph A. Komonchak, trans. Matthew J. O'Connell (Maryknoll, NY: Orbis Books, 1996–2006), 4:95–193; Ricardo Burigana and Giovanni Turbanti, "The Intersession: Preparing the Conclusion of the Council," in *History of Vatican* II, 4:453–615, at 546–59; Mauro Velati, "Completing the Conciliar Agenda," in *History of Vatican II*, 5:185–273, at 211–21.

Nostra Aetate, Vatican II's Declaration on the Relation of the Church to Non-Christian Religions, was not the only conciliar document to refer in positive terms to Jews and members of other non-Christian religions. The Dogmatic Constitution on the Church, *Lumen Gentium* (LG 16), the Decree on the Church's Missionary Activity, *Ad Gentes* (AG 3), and the Pastoral Constitution on the Church in the Modern World, *Gaudium et Spes* (GS 22), made positive references to non-Christian and even nonbelieving people. Those are noteworthy, as they indicate the scope of the council's integration of the theme of interreligious understanding across its teachings. For the first time in the church's history, the institutional church acknowledged other traditions with appreciation and respect.

The innovative nature of *Nostra Aetate* is reflected in the fact that, apart from Scripture references, there is no mention of precedents in the writings of church fathers, conciliar decrees, papal teachings, or other ecclesiastical documents. Nor is there any reference to the Catholic theological tradition. This lack of precedent and the long tradition of what Jules Isaac called "the teaching of contempt" made it difficult for some council fathers to accept the document.[2] Today some still use this lack of precedent, and the fact that *Nostra Aetate* is a declaration and not a constitution, to question the document's authority, or at least the extent of that authority.[3] Others, perhaps most, point to its fundamental quality as a turning point in providing the foundation for a new body of church teaching.[4]

[2] Jules Isaac, *L'enseignement du mépris: Vérité historique et mythes théologiques* (Paris: Fasquelle, 1962); English translation: *The Teaching of Contempt: The Christian Roots of Anti-Semitism*, trans. Helen Weaver (New York: Holt, Rinehart and Winston, 1964), esp. 21–35.

[3] Gavin D'Costa, *Catholic Doctrines on the Jewish People after Vatican II* (Oxford: Oxford University Press, 2019), 7–14, esp. 7–8.

[4] See Philip Cunningham's response, "Gavin D'Costa, *Catholic Doctrines on the Jewish People after Vatican II*," *Studies in Christian*

So, what was in *Nostra Aetate*? We turn to the text to let it speak to us: "In our day, when people are drawing more closely together and the bonds of friendship between different peoples are being strengthened, the church examines more carefully its relations with non-Christian religions. Ever aware of its duty to foster unity and charity among individuals, and even among nations, it reflects at the outset on what people have in common and what tends to bring them together" (NA 1). Thus, the document opens with a look to the larger world beyond the council hall, beyond the Catholic Church itself. The year of its publication, 1965, marked twenty years since the end of the Second World War, which saw the Shoah—the systematic extermination of one-third of the Jewish people—and years of destruction that tore the world asunder and left tens of millions homeless. This was a world in which colonial empires were dying and new nations emerging. *Nostra Aetate* notes that people are now drawing closer together and that the church has a task to foster unity.

The text notes, "People look to their different religions for an answer to the unsolved riddles of human existence. The problems that weigh heavily on people's hearts are the same today as in past ages. . . . What is the ultimate mystery, beyond human explanation, which embraces our entire existence, from which we take our origin and towards which we tend?" (NA 1). *Nostra Aetate* uses the word "mystery" five times.[5] It thus places its reflection on the church's relation to non-Christian religions and the Jewish people in the

Jewish Relations 15, no. 1 (2020): 1–14, esp. 3–5. See also Massimo Faggioli, "*Nostra Aetate* after Fifty Years: History, Not Only Memory, of Vatican II," https://www.abc.net.au/religion/nostra-aetate-after-fifty-years-history-not-only-memory-of-vatic/10097702.

[5] On the theme of "mystery" in *Nostra Aetate,* see Gerald O'Collins, *The Second Vatican Council on Other Religions* (Oxford: Oxford University Press, 2014), 105–8.

context of God's own self, the "mystery . . . which embraces our entire existence" (NA 1).

The text continues, alluding to traditional religions and commenting in general terms on the perennial intuition of "a hidden power which lies behind the course of nature and the events of human life" (NA 2). It then briefly describes some of the central elements in Hinduism and Buddhism. While limited in scope, the tone is positive. The paragraph concludes: "The church, therefore, urges its sons and daughters to enter with prudence and charity into discussion and collaboration with members of other religions. Let Christians, while witnessing to their own faith and way of life, acknowledge, preserve, and encourage the spiritual and moral truths found among non-Christians, together with their social life and culture" (NA 2). This call to dialogue and collaboration is new in the history of official church teaching.

Nostra Aetate 3 turns to Muslims, acknowledging religious commonalities between Christians and Muslims. It closes with an acknowledgment of historical enmity between Christians and Muslims and ends with an entreaty: "The sacred council now pleads with all to forget the past and urges that a sincere effort be made to achieve mutual understanding; for the benefit of all, let them together preserve and promote peace, liberty, social justice, and moral values" (NA 3). Once again, we see the call to dialogue and collaboration, implying that we walk with the religious "other" as equals.

Nostra Aetate 4, the most well-developed section of the Declaration, treats the relationship between Christians and Jews. It begins, "Sounding the depths of the mystery which is the church, this sacred council remembers the spiritual ties which link the people of the new covenant to the stock of Abraham." Paragraph 4 elaborates some ways in which the church is inextricably related to the Jewish people, whom it calls "that people with whom God in his inexpressible mercy established the ancient covenant." *Nostra Aetate* mentions opposition to Jesus by some Jews, but goes on to state, "Even so, the apostle Paul maintains that the Jews remain very dear to God, for the sake of the patriarchs, since God does not take back the gifts bestowed or the choice he made [Rom 11:28–29]." *Nostra Aetate* affirms that the Jews remain in covenant with God.

The document looks to future efforts of joint historical and theological reflection: "Since Christians and Jews have such a common spiritual heritage, this sacred council wishes to encourage and further mutual understanding and appreciation. This can be achieved, especially, by way of biblical and theological enquiry and through friendly discussions" (NA 4). Again, there is an invitation to explore together the sources of history and religious traditions. Never before had such a call been issued.

Nostra Aetate then turns to the question of the responsibility for the death of Jesus. The term "deicide," present in earlier drafts, had been removed after long and often bitter debate. However, the teaching of the document is clear:

> Even though the Jewish authorities and those who followed their lead pressed for the death of Christ (see Jn 19:6), neither all Jews indiscriminately at that time, nor Jews today, can be charged with the crimes committed during his passion. It is true that the church is the new people of God, yet the Jews should not be spoken of as rejected or accursed as if this followed from holy scripture. Consequently, all must take care, lest in catechizing or in the preaching of the word of God, they teach anything which is not in accord with the truth of the Gospel message or the spirit of Christ.
>
> Indeed, the church reproves every form of persecution against whomsoever it may be directed. Remembering, then, its common heritage with the Jews and moved not by any political consideration, but solely by the

> religious motivation of Christian charity, it deplores all hatreds, persecutions, displays of antisemitism levelled at any time or from any source against the Jews.

Nostra Aetate 4 closes with a reminder that the church is to preach "the cross of Christ as the sign of God's universal love and the source of all grace."

Four substantive shifts from previous tradition are found in paragraph 4 on the church's relation to the Jewish people. First, the council underlines the "spiritual ties" between the church, a people of the new covenant, and the descendants of Abraham. The relationship with the Jewish people is intrinsic to Christian identity. The work of dialogue is essential to that which makes us Christian. Second, there is the understanding that the church is in covenant with God *because* of the Jews, drawing "nourishment from that good olive tree onto which the wild olive branches of the Gentiles have been grafted." Third, for the first time, a church document explicitly condemns and deplores anti-Semitism in all its forms. Fourth, as with earlier comments in relation to other religions, there is the call to dialogue and collaboration.[6]

Nostra Aetate 5 moves to a more general reflection on the relation between God and humankind: "People's relation to God the Father and their relation to other women and men are so dependent on each other that the Scripture says: 'they who do not love, do not know God' (1 Jn 4:8)." The declaration concludes with a statement deploring any kind of discrimination against people or any harassment of them because of their race, color, condition of life, or religion. "Accordingly, following the footsteps of the holy apostles Peter and Paul, this sacred council earnestly begs the Christian faithful to 'conduct themselves well among the

[6] Faggioli, "*Nostra Aetate* after Fifty Years," 1.1.

Gentiles' (1 Pet 2:12) and if possible, as far as depends on them, to be at peace with all people (see Rom 12:18) and in that way to be true daughters and sons of the Father who is in heaven (see Mt 5:45)." *Nostra Aetate* has a breathtaking reach, looking outward to the perennial and universal presence of divine mystery and the human quest for meaning. It is daring in its positive appraisal of non-Christian religions and its implied sense of mutuality and call to dialogue and collaboration, inferring that the religions need one another in their search for the Divine and in their labor of creating a world of justice.

The Reception of *Nostra Aetate*

Nostra Aetate brought new ways of teaching, working, and exploring together what it means to stand together before God and each other. The origins of this development go back at least to the nineteenth and early twentieth centuries with movements of interreligious understanding such as those exemplified by the 1893 Parliament of World Religions, *philosémitisme*,[7] and *ressourcement*,[8] collaboration among Central European scholars,[9] and documents

[7] Olivier Rota, *Essai sur le philosémitisme catholique entre le premier et le second concile de Vatican: Un parcours dans la modernité chrétienne* (Arras: Artois Presses Université, 2012).

[8] E.g., "Le Père Joseph Bonsirven: un parcours fait d'ombres et de lumières," *Archives Juives* 40 (2007/1): 30–44; Anthony O'Mahony, "Louis Massignon: A Catholic Encounter with Islam and the Middle East," in *God's Mirror: Renewal and Engagement in French Catholic Intellectual Culture in the Mid-Twentieth Century*, ed. Katherine Davies and Toby Garfitt (New York: Fordham University Press, 2015), 230–51. For a list of those whose work contributed to new approaches among Roman Catholics toward Hinduism and Buddhism, see Jacques Scheuer, "The Dialogue with the Traditions of India and the Far East," *Gregorianum* 87, no. 4 (2006): 797–809, at 800.

[9] John Connelly, *From Enemy to Brother: The Revolution in*

such as the "Address to the Churches (The Ten Points of Seelisberg)" (1947) and "The Apeldoorn Theses" (1961).[10] With its global institutional reach, *Nostra Aetate* represented the culmination of that work and an opening to further horizons.

In 1964, during the council, Pope Paul VI established the Pontifical Commission for Religious Relations with the Jews, within the Secretariat (now Dicastery) for Promoting Christian Unity. In 1974 he established the Pontifical Council (now Dicastery) for Interreligious Dialogue. Already in the 1960s, Catholic monks and nuns had been meeting with monastics from other international traditions. The year 1994 saw the formation of Dialogue Interreligieux Monastique—Monastic Interreligious Dialogue.[11]

A body of documents has been produced by the dicasteries for Relations with the Jews and for Interreligious Dialogue and their collaborators. In 2015, the Commission for Religious Relations with the Jews published "The Gifts and the Calling of God Are Irrevocable (Rom 11:29): A Reflection on Theological Questions Pertaining to Catholic-Jewish Relations on the Occasion of the 50th Anniversary of '*Nostra Aetate*' (No. 4)."[12] And on February 4, 2019, Pope

---

Catholic Teaching on the Jews, 1933–1965 (Cambridge, MA: Harvard University Press, 2012), esp. 1–10.

[10] The "Address to the Churches (The Ten Points of Seelisberg)" was one of the first documents produced by Christians, with the help of Jews, to confront the questions raised by the Shoah (Holocaust). The "Apeldoorn Theses" summarized the thinking of participants in the Apeldoorn Conference on a variety of questions concerning relations between Christians and Jews. These and other precursor documents can be accessed at the website of the Council of Centers on Jewish-Christian Relations, https://ccjr.us/dialogika-resources/documents-and-statements/roman-catholic/second-vatican-council/naprecursors.

[11] See www.dimmid.org; see also Fabrice Blée, *The Third Desert: The Story of Monastic Interreligious Dialogue*, trans. William Skudlarek with Mary Grady (Collegeville, MN: Liturgical Press, 2011).

[12] Commission on Religious Relations with the Jews, "'The Gifts

Francis and the Grand Imam of Al-Azhar Ahmad Al-Tayyeb co-signed at Abu Dhabi "A Document on Human Fraternity for World Peace and Living Together."[13]

There has been another kind of teaching embodied in the prophetic gestures and witness of religious leaders, beginning with postconciliar popes. This is exemplified in Pope Paul VI's visit to Israel and Jordan in January 1964, during the council. Pope John Paul II later visited the Great Synagogue of Rome in 1986, and prayed at the Western Wall of the Temple in Jerusalem in 2000, where he inserted between the stones of the Wall the text of a prayer he had recited during the Jubilee Year "Mass of Pardon" in St. Peter's Basilica.[14] Pope Benedict visited several synagogues: Cologne in 2005, the Park East Synagogue in New York City in 2008, and the Great Synagogue in Rome in 2010. Pope Francis embraced Rabbi Abraham Skorka and Sheikh Omar Abboud in Jerusalem during their journey to Israel, Palestine, and Jordan in May 2014. Since 1986, the World Day of Prayer for Peace has been celebrated in Assisi, bringing together religious leaders from around the globe, representing world religious traditions as well as local traditional religions.[15]

Nostra Aetate took on a life of its own. There is now a

---

and Calling of God Are Irrevocable' (Rom 11:29): A Reflection on Theological Questions Pertaining to Catholic-Jewish Relations on the Occasion of the 50th Anniversary of *Nostra Aetate* (no. 4)," http://www.christianunity.va/content/unitacristiani/en/commissione-per-i-rapporti-religiosi-con-l-ebraismo/commissione-per-i-rapporti-religiosi-con-l-ebraismo-crre/documenti-della-commissione/en.html.

[13] Pope Francis and Grand Imam of Al-Azhar, Ahmad Al-Tayeb, "A Document on Human Fraternity for World Peace and Living Together," February 4, 2019.

[14] Cunningham, "Gavin D'Costa," 1–2; Faggioli, "*Nostra Aetate* after Fifty Years," 1.2.

[15] Msgr. Indunil J. Kodithuwakku K., "World Day of Prayer for Peace in Assisi," October 27, 2021, https://www.dicasteryinterreligious.va/35th-anniversary-of-interreligious-meeting-for-peace-in-assisi/.

body of official Catholic teaching that not only denies the age-old charge of deicide, but also reminds Catholic Christians that God's covenant with the Jewish people endures forever.[16] In many countries, that new body of teaching has been translated into religious education materials and collaboration in matters of common concern. In the United States, the study of non-Christian religions and Judaism flourishes in secular and religious colleges and universities, and theological faculties.

The reach of *Nostra Aetate* has extended far beyond Roman Catholic circles. It led to the foundation in 1967 of the International Jewish Committee for Interreligious Consultations (IJCIC) to represent Jews to the Vatican and, later, with other non-Jewish religions and non-Catholic Christian denominations. In 1970 the International Catholic-Jewish Liaison Committee (ILC) was established by the Vatican. Other Christian denominations extended their work, producing their own materials.[17]

The Ways of Dialogue

From what has been said thus far, one might conclude that interfaith or interreligious dialogue is primarily a

[16] For example: The Pontifical Biblical Commission, "The Jewish People and Their Sacred Scriptures in the Christian Bible," May 24, 2001, https://www.vatican.va/roman_curia/congregations/cfaith/pcb_documents/rc_con_cfaith_doc_20020212_popolo-ebraico_en.html; the Commission for Religious Relations with the Jews, "Notes on the Correct Way to Present the Jews and Judaism in Preaching and Catechesis in the Roman Catholic Church," 1985, http://www.christianunity.va/content/unitacristiani/fr/commissione-per-i-rapporti-religiosi-con-l-ebraismo/commissione-per-i-rapporti-religiosi-con-l-ebraismo-crre/documenti-della-commissione/fr/en.html.

[17] For examples of documents from Protestant and Anglican churches and coalitions, see the documentation made available at www.ccjr.us/dialogika-resources/documents-and-statements/protestant-churches.

question of hierarchical and clerical leaders making official pronouncements, issuing documents, or of scholars engaged in academic study and conversation. However, there is much more to this work. In 1984 Pope John Paul II addressed the Pontifical Commission for Interreligious Dialogue on the scope of dialogue, in a text titled "Dialogue and Mission."[18] The same principles were reiterated even more clearly in the 1994 document of the Pontifical Council for Interreligious Dialogue, "Dialogue and Proclamation. It speaks of

a. The *dialogue of life*, where people strive to live in an open and neighborly spirit, sharing their joys and sorrows, their human problems and preoccupations.
b. The *dialogue of action*, in which Christians and others collaborate for the integral development and liberation of people.
c. The *dialogue of theological exchange*, where specialists seek to deepen their understanding of their respective religious heritages, and to appreciate each other's spiritual values.
d. The *dialogue of religious experience*, where persons, rooted in their own religious traditions, share their spiritual riches, for instance, regarding prayer and contemplation, faith, and ways of searching for God or the Absolute.[19]

The "dialogue of theological exchange" might be understood more broadly as a "dialogue of scholarly exchange," for it includes everything from sociology to history, from

[18] John Paul II, "The Attitude of the Church towards the Followers of Other Religions: Reflections and Orientations on Dialogue and Mission," March 3, 1984, https://www.dicasteryinterreligious.va/dialogue-and-mission-1984/.

[19] Pontifical Council for Interreligious Dialogue, "Dialogue and Proclamation," no. 42; See also John Paul II, "Dialogue and Mission," secs. 29–35.

the biblical period to the present. It takes place in seminaries and rabbinical schools, at the Vatican and in national conferences of bishops. It occurs in the meetings of the Council of Centers for Jewish-Christian Relations (CCJR), or the sessions of the International Council for Christians and Jews (ICCJ), or the Abrahamic Forum. But it also takes place in academic, "secular" conferences such as meetings of the American Academy of Religion and the Society of Biblical Literature. It takes place as scholars move back and forth between offices or consult by phone or WhatsApp or Zoom, conferring about their work, and exchanging news about family and friends.

This kind of exchange has transformed the study of the New Testament, early Christianity, and early Judaism. There are now Jews who are recognized experts in the study of the New Testament and early Christianity, and Christians specializing in the study of Judaism.[20] Christianity, like Judaism, is grounded in its foundational (i.e., canonical) texts. How those texts are interpreted makes a difference, not only for understanding the context of Jesus's life and ministry, but also the depictions of conflict between Jesus and Jewish leaders such as the "Pharisees," and the critical events surrounding his death. We remember the ways in which the accusation of "deicide"—the charge that the Jews killed God—was used to legitimate the persecution of Jews and know that this transformation of scholarship does indeed make a difference. Jesus is now understood by many, whether scholars or people in the pews, to be *part* of his very complex and complicated world, not as someone outside his tradition or superseding it.[21]

---

[20] One example of such scholarship is *The Jewish Annotated New Testament*, 2nd ed., ed. Amy-Jill Levine and Marc Zvi Brettler (Oxford: Oxford University Press, 2017).

[21] Mary C. Boys, *Has God Only One Blessing? Judaism as a Source of Christian Self-Understanding* (New York: Paulist Press, 2000), 91–148.

But most people are not scholars or "professionals" in ecumenism, interfaith, or interreligious dialogue. The other three categories outlined in "Dialogue and Proclamation" refer to *everyone*. Every Roman Catholic is called to interfaith, interreligious, and ecumenical dialogue. In the words of "Dialogue and Mission," "No local Church is exempt from this duty, which is made urgent by continuous changes. Because of migrations, travels, social communications and personal choices, believers of different religions and cults easily meet each other and often live together."[22] Believers of different religions easily meet one another in their new contexts, but those encounters may be fraught with stereotypes or memories of negative experiences from their former homelands.

My favorite phrase in this context is "dialogue of life"—"where people strive to live in an open and neighborly spirit, sharing their joys and sorrows, their human problems and preoccupations." I think about my neighborhood, with its large Muslim population. Parts of New York City are home to well-established Muslim communities. But the Muslim community in central Brooklyn is made up of new arrivals. Many are frightened because they might be undocumented or because of the anti-Islamic prejudice, even hatred, that is so prevalent in US society. New immigrants must often work too hard and too many hours to engage in extra activities, including interfaith or interreligious dialogue. But there is the "dialogue of life," a spirit of neighborliness, and I enjoy the greetings on the street. Conversations with shopkeepers often become opportunities for conversation about our religious traditions.

There is also a "dialogue of action" in which "Christians and others collaborate for the integral development and liberation of people." Collaboration happens on many levels, as we work together for the social and physical well-being

[22] John Paul II, "Dialogue and Mission," no. 3.

of our people. Think of those iconic photos of Dr. Martin Luther King Jr., Rabbi Abraham Joshua Heschel, and Fr. Daniel Berrigan marching in Selma, where so many people travelled hundreds of miles by bus to join local African Americans and whites in the struggle for racial justice. Together they risked arrest, beatings, jail, even death.

More modestly, in the realm most of us inhabit, there is collaboration on a wide range of social issues and projects: immigration, soup kitchens, care of creation, voting rights, gun violence, and more.[23] The Interfaith Coalition of Brooklyn organized a series of silent prayer vigils early in 2017 in response to the "Muslim Ban," a ban on immigration from "Muslim" countries. This was a deeply personal action for all of us because a large percentage of people in the neighborhood, primarily Catholics and Muslims, are undocumented. Our friends are vulnerable, and the lives of many families continue to be threatened. We support a parish food pantry that feeds all who come. We hold study sessions, sharing the riches of our traditions. We do this *because* we are Christians, Jews, Muslims, whose traditions teach us to study our sacred texts, and to care for the poor, the stranger, the vulnerable, the oppressed.

Finally, there is the "dialogue of religious experience where persons, rooted in their own religious traditions, share their spiritual riches, with regard to prayer and contemplation, faith and ways of searching for God or the Absolute." Beyond the monastic context, there are also gatherings for meditation, or for Thanksgiving services, so meaningful in the US context. Jews and Muslims in our co-

---

[23] The Center for Interfaith Relations in the diocese of Louisville, Kentucky, recently brought together people from the religious traditions represented in the city for a service in the Cathedral of the Assumption to address the gun violence that erupted in that city on April 10, 2023. See "Broken Hearts, Anxious Minds: Commitment to a Healthy Community," https://www.centerforinterfaithrelations.org/.

alition often join our parish congregation for the celebration of Our Lady of Guadalupe. While not joining in the prayer itself, our neighbors stand with us in solidarity, encouraging us in our own religious practice. And then there are interfaith *iftars* when Muslims welcome family and friends each evening to break the Ramadan fast. We *are* becoming family and friends, learning about practices of prayer and fasting in each other's tradition. In the process, we come to understand and treasure our own traditions more deeply.

This is hard work. Fabrice Blée likens interreligious dialogue to a desert.[24] Think about the experience of hiking in the desert or even walking a mountain trail. There is a pull of sand or gravel on your boots, the sun and heat, or perhaps cold rain, thirst, hunger. When conditions are difficult, one may need to collaborate with fellow hikers to make it to the end. Hikers may need to depend on the kindliness of strangers and be willing to go beyond familiar landmarks. On the "path" of dialogue, we not only meet one another in new respect and friendship, but we also join to confront the social problems that threaten all of us, both human beings and the planet itself.[25]

The website of Oasis, an organization for interreligious dialogue based in Venice, Italy, says that interreligious dialogue "involves intercultural dialogue because religious experience is always lived and expressed through the medium of culture; not merely at the theological and spiritual level, but also at the political, economic, and social ones."[26] Dialogue requires letting go of old preconceptions and assumptions, letting the other be as she/he/they are. It means "deepening love for the distinctiveness of the . . . other

[24] Blée, *The Third Desert*, 8–9.

[25] James Fredericks, "The Dialogue of Fraternity: Pope Francis's Approach to Religious Engagement," *Commonweal* 144, no. 6 (March 24, 2017): 10–11.

[26] Oasis Center, http://www.oasiscenter.eu/about-us.

because of their edifying ways of walking with God."[27]

Interreligious understanding is a kind of hospitality.[28] Hospitality is not always comfortable. To welcome the other in interreligious dialogue means to expose oneself to the risk of de-centering one's own self-understanding as Jew, as Christian, as Muslim, Buddhist, Sikh, traditional practitioner, and so on. For genuine encounter to occur, host and guest must "attend to questions about motivation and perception, questions which have awkwardly affective as well as more purely cognitive dimensions. If the desire that draws human beings into relationship is not to stop short at an uncritical isolation, it has to be tempered by self-knowledge and careful discernment."[29]

We saw how the opening words of *Nostra Aetate* 4 place Christian-Jewish relations at the heart of the church's own identity, a "mystery," suggesting a never-ending quest for what is ultimately only revealed by God. As Gordis and Phan remind us, "We seek to understand more about ourselves and our world than we can possibly comprehend. Our reach exceeds our grasp."[30] The journey into mystery suggests that ecumenical, interfaith, and interreligious dialogue (including Catholic-Jewish relations) are a matter of spiritual experience. The word "mystery" invites us into contemplation of the depth of God's own self, of our traditions, and the vast

---

[27] Philip A. Cunningham, *Seeking Shalom: The Journey to Right Relationship between Catholics and Jews* (Grand Rapids: Wm. B. Eerdmans, 2015), 249.

[28] Michael Barnes, *Theology and the Dialogue of Religions* (Cambridge: Cambridge University Press, 2002), 62–64; *Waiting on Grace: A Theology of Dialogue* (Oxford: Oxford University Press, 2020), 15–45.

[29] Barnes, *Waiting on Grace*, 21–22.

[30] David M. Gordis and Peter C. Phan, "Catholics and Jews Looking Ahead," in *Toward the Future: Essays on Catholic-Jewish Relations in Memory of Rabbi León Klenicki*, ed. Celia M. Deutsch, Eugene J. Fisher, and James Rudin (New York: Paulist Press, 2013), 215–23, at 221.

space opened up by the process of encounter and conversation we engage in individually, as well as through communal practices of prayer and meditation, reading and listening to sacred texts in our communities in the context of study and worship. Interfaith and interreligious dialogue can take the practitioner beyond the community's established boundaries to engage others as co-partners in encounter with the divine, in care of humankind and of the Earth itself.

Why bother? After all, the journey is sometimes uncomfortable and fraught with risk. Is not the work of ecumenism and interfaith and interreligious understanding a luxury for those who have "time" to engage? We should bother because these religious "others" are neighbors, both metaphorically and literally. Often in our complex and intermarried world, they are family members.

Interfaith and interreligious work is important because 85 percent or more of the world's people are affiliated in one way or another with a religious tradition. In recent decades, brutal wars, such as that between Serbia and Bosnia, have been fought along religious lines (Orthodox Christianity and Islam). Globally, no religious community can claim clean hands in the violence of past decades. Members of all our communities have perpetrated violence in the name of God.

Religion can indeed be a path to violence, legitimating all manner of injustice against the innocent. But religion can also provide ways to peace and justice.[31] In 2011 the UN inaugurated its first annual World Interfaith Harmony Week. There are national groups such as the Interfaith Encounter Association in Israel, and international groups such as Religions for Peace and the Parliament of World Religions. Local churches such as the Roman Catholic Diocese of El Paso collaborate with interfaith partners to

---

[31] Peter C. Phan, *Being Religious Interreligiously; Asian Perspectives on Interfaith Dialogue* (Maryknoll, NY: Orbis Books, 2004), 186–209.

help people organize to meet the vast array of needs challenging communities on the Mexican-US border.[32] These efforts to work together for justice and care for the Earth are grounded in our traditions—Indigenous, Christian, Jewish, Muslim, Hindu, Buddhist, Sikh, Jain, Daoist. People from the whole spectrum of religious traditions join nonaffiliated people in the effort.

Challenges

Nearly sixty years ago, *Nostra Aetate* offered daring new perspectives on the church's relationship to non-Christian religions, especially in relation to the Jewish people. I have given a broad and general view of its reception, largely focused on the United States. That reception has exceeded the boundaries of the Roman Catholic Church and even those of institutional religion. Various religious traditions are being studied in a multitude of contexts. In this country and elsewhere, people of different traditions collaborate in a multitude of ways on issues pertaining to immigration, voters' rights, care of creation, and more. Scholars here and abroad continue to probe the historical and theological questions regarding origins, Christology, and ecclesiology. In Jewish-Christian dialogue, scholars are probing the theological significance of the Land of Israel.[33]

At the same time, interfaith and interreligious work faces serious challenges. One of the primary challenges for US Catholic engagement is the polarization of society and of church. How do we engage with people who differ from us politically? How do we reach across socioeconomic, class, ethnic, and racial divides in respect and, even, hospitality?

---

[32] National Catholic Reporter, "For Synod Listening Sessions, US Bishops Turn to Community Organizers," January 3, 2023.

[33] Philip A. Cunningham, Ruth Langer, and Jesper Svartvik, eds., *Enabling Dialogue about the Land* (New York: Paulist Press, 2020).

Even more difficult, how do we reach across divides within our church, with respect for those who have different understandings of Catholic identity? Our inability to confront these fundamental questions threatens the continuation of interfaith and interreligious engagement. That same polarization makes the work even more important.

In this context we often face a lack of leadership by many of our bishops and pastoral leaders, whether clergy or lay, despite the hope offered by engagement in the synodal way, and by the encouragement and commitment of Popes Paul VI, John Paul II, Benedict XVI, and Francis. In this country, the vibrant institutional commitment to ecumenism and interfaith and interreligious dialogue of the first three decades after the council has steadily diminished. So, while it is true that a great deal of outreach remains present in many areas, the leadership no longer comes from the offices of the United States Conference of Catholic Bishops (USCCB), or even most of our dioceses.

To be sure, the USCCB's Committee on Ecumenical and Interreligious Affairs has held regular meetings over the past sixty years with representatives of the National Council of Synagogues, the Orthodox Union, and now the Modern Orthodox Group. On November 18, 2022, the committee issued a "Recommitment to Relationship with the Jewish Community,"[34] with reference to the escalation of anti-Semitism in this country. The leadership of more sustained work, however, has moved to the many centers and institutes located on college and university campuses, as well as in some seminaries.

The work being done in those venues is excellent. However, most seminary and pastoral education programs do not

---

[34] United States Conference of Catholic Bishops, "USCCB's Committee on Ecumenical and Interreligious Affairs Emphasizes Recommitment to Relationship with Jewish Community," November 28, 2022.

integrate into the training of those who will lead parishes and other grassroots communities the church's teaching on ecumenism, Jewish-Christian relations, and interreligious relations. If courses are offered, they are often electives. In the minds of too many, ecumenism and interfaith and interreligious relations remain "something extra," "something for the specialists." Bishops and pastoral workers, whether clergy or lay, are often overwhelmed by the demands of ministry in the extraordinarily complex context of twenty-first-century US Catholic life. Ecumenical, interfaith, and interreligious work can seem extraneous to the demands of holding together communities beset by challenges ranging from the ongoing ravages of sex abuse scandals to poverty and immigration and racism, and the structuring of parish life. Many of our communities are simply exhausted, given the impact of the pandemic. Yet this is even more reason why we need pastoral leaders whose formation integrates interreligious relations in the same way it integrates—or should integrate—social justice and the care of creation, or liturgy, Scripture, and fundamental theology. We need leaders who can translate the work being done in official circles or academic arenas into the lives of grassroots communities.[35]

Another challenge is the dramatic escalation of anti-Semitism evident online, in personal and political speech, preaching, vandalism, in-person attacks, the bullying of children, and physical violence.[36] The escalation culminated in the mass murder of eleven Jewish worshippers at the Tree of Life Synagogue in Pittsburgh on October 27,

---

[35] For a one-volume resource, see *The Jewish Annotated New Testament*, cited in footnote 21. See *The Pharisees*, ed. Joseph Sievers and Amy-Jill Levine (Grand Rapids: Wm. B. Eerdmans, 2021).

[36] See American Jewish Committee, "The State of Antisemitism in America 2022: Insight and Analysis," April 14, 2023, https://www.ajc.org/AntisemitismReport2022.

2018.[37] In the United States, as elsewhere, anti-Semitism is linked to the intensification of racism.[38] Conspiracy theories, ancient tropes of deicide, and more are alive and well. Some of our parishioners and even our clergy believe these toxic stereotypes. Many of the same challenges that face Jews at this point in our history also face other religious minorities, such as Muslims, Hindus, and Sikhs, as well as Black, Latino, Pacific Islander, Indigenous, and Asian people. Religious bigotry is entwined with racism and the tropes of geopolitics.[39]

The hard work of welcoming others with everything that makes them different brings us up against our limitations, personal as well as communal. The experience of these limitations can be painful and humbling—so we walk the desert path, we welcome one another, we cook food for a communal feast. We pray in vigil in solidarity with our brothers and sisters threatened with deportation. We work together in ways great and small to care for our fragile Mother Earth. We study and learn the traditions of people who once seemed strange, other. We sit together in silence before the One who is All in All, who is the Other, and yet who is infinitely near.[40]

---

[37] Isabel Fattal, "A Brief History of Anti-Semitic Violence in America," *The Atlantic*, October 28, 2018.

[38] Amy Kaplan, "The Old 'New Anti-Semitism' and Resurgent White Supremacy," *Middle East Report* 283 (2017): 10–15. Kaplan focuses particularly on the hyper-Zionism of some evangelical Christian and white supremacist groups; see also Jonathan A. Greenblatt, "Fighting Hate in the Era of Coronavirus," *Horizons: A Journal of International Relations and Sustainable Development* 17 (2020): 208–21. The elision of racism and anti-Semitism has roots in the eighteenth century; see Mary Boys, *Redeeming Our Sacred Story: The Death of Jesus and Relations between Jews and Christians* (New York: Paulist Press, 2013), 109–11; on racism among Catholics in the years before World War II, including the issue of eugenics, see Connelly, *From Enemy to Brother*, 36–95.

[39] Greenblatt, "Fighting Hate."

[40] Barnes, *Theology and the Dialogue of Religions*, 205–29.

Why bother? We "bother" because God is bigger than us all, infinitely more than any tradition can contain or describe, and the needs of our world exceed the capacities of any one group. We need to cherish our traditions and our identities. We need boundaries to help us know who we are. And we need to reach across those boundaries to know who we are, to build a better world, a place of safety and justice for all, indeed, to save the world that all of us believe—in one way or another—has been given into our keeping.

9

The Spirituality of the Second Vatican Council

Gerald O'Collins, SJ

It left me sad some years ago to hear a leading theologian dismiss "spirituality" as "giving trees a hug" and indulging similar forms of exuberant behavior. He failed to recognize that spirituality is primarily the *practice* of a prayerful, devout, and disciplined Christian life. Such practice can only be highly desirable and valuable.

Spirituality also points to the *teaching* of those who reflect upon the sources of such prayerful, devout, and disciplined practice and the various forms it takes. The classic French *Dictionnaire de Spiritualité* (1932–95) took over fifteen thousand pages and more than sixty years to produce its monument of scholarship. We also find a rich, if different, example of such teaching in the Second Vatican Council (1962–65).

The council issued no specific document that would describe Christian or Catholic spirituality. But, taken together, its sixteen documents offered essential guidelines on how we should live our *baptismal* call to holiness as set out in paragraphs 39 to 42 of the Dogmatic Constitution on the Church

(*Lumen Gentium*). These spiritual guidelines include at least *eight* invitations: be centered on Jesus and his presence; be liturgical; be biblical; serve others in a priestly, prophetic, and pastoral way; remain committed to those in need; be penitent reformers; be attentive to the Blessed Virgin Mary and the saints; and be in friendly dialogue with all people.

Be Centered on Jesus and His Presence

The documents of the council included no particular text dedicated to Jesus the Christ. Rather, his presence pervaded the teaching and proceedings of the council. The final document, the Pastoral Constitution on the Church in the Modern World (*Gaudium et Spes*), summed up the central vision of Vatican II and its spirituality: "The Lord is the goal of human history, the focal point of the desires of history and civilization, the center of humanity, the joy of all hearts, and the fulfillment of all aspirations" (GS 45).

"The joy of all hearts" brings to mind a chorale of Johann Sebastian Bach, for which Robert Bridges supplied the words: "Jesu, Joy of man's desiring, / Holy wisdom, love most bright. / Drawn by thee, our souls aspiring / Soar to uncreated light." "Joy of all hearts" could also summon up a Christmas carol by Isaac Watts, "Joy to the World," and the "Ode to Joy" from the Ninth Symphony of Ludwig van Beethoven.

The lyrical image of this picture of Jesus, taken from a Vatican II document called "Joy and Hope" (*Gaudium et Spes*), could easily be transposed into prayer: "Jesus, you are the goal of human history. Jesus, you are the focal point of our desires. Jesus, you are the joy of my heart. Jesus, you are the fullness of all my yearnings."

Pope St. Paul VI had anticipated this language of *Gaudium et Spes* when addressing the council on September 29, 1963. Pope St. John XXIII had convoked Vatican II and lived long enough to open the council and preside at its first session. His successor, Paul VI, took over the task of leading the council for three more sessions. On the opening day of the second session, he asked, "Where does our path start? What course should it follow? What goal must it set? Three essential questions in all simplicity. There is only a single answer to them, Christ. Christ our principle; Christ our way and our leader; Christ our hope and our goal."[1]

What Paul VI said in September 1963 easily turns into prayer: "Christ, you are our way and our leader. Christ, you are our hope and our goal." This is the way to pray; this is the way to live, with Christ our way, our hope, and our goal.

Vatican II offered a vivid picture of what being centered on Jesus Christ meant for the workings of a general council of the church. At the general "congregations" or meetings of each of its four sessions (1962–65), a daily Eucharist opened the proceedings in St. Peter's Basilica, Rome. Each day the Book of the Gospels was carried in and solemnly enthroned by a deacon. That book symbolized the risen Jesus, invisibly but dynamically present at the heart of the council to preside over all the liturgical celebrations, speeches, debates, and deliberations.

The very first document to be promulgated at the council, the 1963 Constitution on the Sacred Liturgy (*Sacrosanctum Concilium*), included a brilliant passage that listed *five* ways in which Christ remains present to us when we meet to pray together:

---

[1] Paul VI, Solenne inizio della seconda sessione del concilio ecumenico Vaticano II, September 29, 1963. The original Italian reads thus: "Da dove prenderà l'avvio, Venerabili Fratelli, il nostro cammino? E poi che via si dovrà seguire? . . . Infine, quale traguardo si dovrà prestabilire al nostro percorso? . . . Queste tre domande, che all'intelletto sono così elementari . . . hanno un'unica risposta . . . Cristo è il nostro principio, Cristo è la nostra guida e la nostra via, Cristo è la nostra speranza e la nostra meta." https://www.vatican.va/content/paul-vi/it/speeches/1963/documents/hf_p-vi_spe_19630929_concilio-vaticano-ii.html.

> Christ is always present in his church, especially in liturgical celebrations. He is present in the sacrifice of the Mass both in the person of his minister . . . and most of all in the eucharistic species. By his power he is present in the sacraments so that when anybody baptizes it is really Christ himself who baptizes. He is present in his word since it is he himself who speaks when the holy scriptures are read in church. Lastly, he is present when the church prays and sings, for he has promised "where two or three are gathered together in my name there am I in the midst of them" (Mt 18:20). (SC 7)

In short, Christ is never absent when his church meets in worship but always present in a variety of ways.

First, the ordained ministers do not represent an absent Christ; rather, they are living signs of the invisible but powerfully present Christ who constantly intercedes for us all. This led Thomas Aquinas to say that "Christ alone is the true priest, but others are His ministers."[2] The 1994 *Catechism of the Catholic Church* quoted these words of Aquinas, and so brought out the ever-active nature of Christ's priesthood (CCC 1545). At Mass, our spiritual gaze allows us to pass through the celebrant to the presence of Jesus Christ himself.

As the second mode of presence, *Sacrosanctum Concilium* points to the uniquely special presence in, with, and under the consecrated bread and wine. The Eucharist forms the most intimate and powerful way that Christ becomes present. Faced with the awesome beauty of this eucharistic presence, Aquinas turned the prose of his theology into the poetry of the Latin hymns he composed for the Feast

---

[2] St. Thomas Aquinas, *Super epistolam B. Pauli ad Hebraeos lectura (Commentary on the Epistle to the Hebrews),* trans. Fabian R. Larcher, OP, 7-4: Heb 7:20–28, §368, https://isidore.co/aquinas/SSHebrews.htm.

of Corpus Christi. In the translation by Gerard Manley Hopkins, this is the first verse of the *Adoro te devote*: "Godhead here in hiding, whom I do adore. / Masked by these bare shadows, shape and nothing more. / See, Lord, at thy service low lies here a heart. / Lost, all lost in wonder at the God thou art."

To support the third mode of Christ's presence, a presence through the sacraments other than the Eucharist, *Sacrosanctum Concilium* 7 cites St. Augustine of Hippo (d. 430). No matter who administers the sacraments visibly, Christ is always present as the primary agent. In Augustine's words, "[baptism] that . . . was given by Paul, and that which was given by Peter, is Christ's" (*Tractates on the Gospel of John* 5.18).[3] Through baptism, Christ introduces men and women into the new family of God. Through the other sacraments, he becomes present to care for them in their basic spiritual needs.

The fourth mode of Christ's presence takes us back to the ancient practice at Mass when the Book of the Gospels is solemnly carried in a procession that evokes his entering the assembly. The deacon or priest traces a sign of Christ's cross on the Book of the Gospels, and then makes a sign of the cross on his forehead, mouth, and heart before proclaiming or singing the text. After the Gospel is announced, the congregation addresses the risen Christ, invisibly but truly present *through the inspired text*, by saying, "Glory to you, O Lord." Then, like the deacon or priest, they too make the sign of the cross on their forehead, mouth, and heart. By their bodily posture, gestures, and words, they too acknowledge his being present to them through the inspired Word of God. As *Sacrosanctum Concilium* puts it later, "In the liturgy . . . Christ is still proclaiming his gospel" (SC 33).

The *assembled community* that "prays and sings" to-

---

[3] Augustine of Hippo, *Tractates on the Gospel of John* 5.18, https://www.newadvent.org/fathers/1701005.htm.

gether forms the context for the fifth mode of Christ's presence. Here the constitution appropriately cites his promise: "where two or three are gathered together in my name, I am there in the midst of them." His presence is realized in every assembly of his followers, even in a tiny gathering of two or three persons. When they reach out to each other with love and friendship, this will allow the risen Christ to transform their lives and communities. His presence will serve to banish the partisan conflicts and divisions that have afflicted many assemblies of Catholic and other Christian disciples. Culture war politics remain incompatible with the Christ who makes himself present to all his brothers and sisters.

From the early centuries of Christianity, the followers of Jesus have recognized other means of his presence. The altar, a central focus for celebrating the Eucharist, brings us the presence of Christ, "the priest, victim, *and altar*" of a once-and-for-all sacrifice to the Father. Think too of the great Easter candle, which symbolizes Christ the risen light of the world. It manifests his presence not only at the celebration of the Eucharist but also at baptism and funerals. Eastern Christians give a special place to icons in their spirituality. These three sacred representations—altars, Easter candles, and icons—signal the presence of the glorious Christ, who accompanies us at worship and in life.

Be Actively Liturgical in Your Spirituality

Through its teaching on the liturgy and in other ways, Vatican II highlighted the presence of Christ for the life of his followers. Being Christ-centered in our spirituality necessarily means finding the heart of our existence in the church's gathering for worship.

It comes as no surprise to find *Sacrosanctum Concilium* urging pastors to "ensure that the faithful take part fully aware of what they are doing, actively engaged in the rite and enriched by it" (SC 11). This document speaks twenty-three times of "participation" in the liturgy, and it means "that all the faithful should be led to take that full, conscious, and active part in liturgical celebrations which is demanded by the very nature of the liturgy" (SC 14).

When I was a boy, we were taught that "you fulfill your Sunday obligation by arriving at Mass in time for the offertory." The Liturgy of the Word was discounted. What really mattered was attending the Liturgy of the Eucharist and receiving Holy Communion. In any case, during my early years, the Scriptures were still being read or (occasionally) sung in Latin. The overwhelming majority of the congregation knew no Latin. At best they followed the epistle and Gospel in the English missals they brought to church. Very many filled up the time quietly reciting the rosary or engaged with other personal devotions.

Sacrosanctum Concilium knows what truly active *participation* in the Eucharist can bring: "The liturgy is the summit toward which the activity of the church is directed; it is also the source from which all its power flows" (SC 10). Ideally, the activity of Christians should always be directed toward the Sunday Eucharist, the spiritual highpoint of the week's story. The Eucharist should also be the source of power for their actively following Christ for the week to come.

What is at stake here could well prompt this prayer: "Jesus, week by week let me direct my life toward our Sunday Mass, offering everything to you, and with the strength of the Holy Spirit praising the Father and praying for the needs of the world. Jesus, let me leave the Sunday Eucharist constantly empowered by the Spirit to live the coming week as your true disciple."

Be Biblical: Constantly Draw Light and Life from the Scriptures

Many scholars judge the key document issued by Vatican II to be the Dogmatic Constitution on Divine Revelation (*Dei Verbum*), promulgated on November 18, 1965. In its final chapter, *Dei Verbum* "forcefully and specifically" exhorted all the Christian faithful "to learn 'the surpassing knowledge of Jesus Christ' (Phil 3:8) by frequently reading of the divine scriptures. 'Ignorance of the scriptures is ignorance of Christ' " (DV 25).

During my early years at the Gregorian University in Rome (1973–2006), I enjoyed the company of Fr. Carlo Maria Martini. At first, he lived right across the street as rector of the Biblical Institute. Then in 1978 he moved to the Gregorian University as rector, and two years later began his ministry as archbishop of Milan. Right from our first contacts, it struck me how Martini constantly drew light and life from the Bible.

His whole existence and way of going about things were utterly biblical. He regularly began committee meetings by reading a few verses of Scripture and inviting those present to share a moment or two of silence before they took up the agenda. Martini consistently put his day-to-day work under the word of God. Those who shared life with him at the Biblical Institute, at the Gregorian, and in Milan felt the blessing of working with someone who expected to be persistently guided and strengthened by the inspired word of God.

In season and out of season, Martini encouraged others to live in the light of the Bible. He excelled in drawing from the Scripture something appropriate for any situation. When Pope John Paul I died suddenly in September 1978 after only a month in office, Martini preached at a funeral Mass in the Church of the Gesù (Rome). He reflected on a text about John the Baptist: "He was a burning and shining lamp, and for a while you were content to rejoice in his light" (John 5:35). Martini applied the text squarely to his congregation. They had delighted in the light and life communicated through the short pontificate of "the smiling pope," he told them. But would they continue to manifest in their lives the blessing which the late John Paul I (now Blessed John Paul I) had brought them?

Martini went deeply into that one verse from John's Gospel and related it to all of us present at the Eucharist. You cannot preach this kind of biblical homily without constantly reading, studying, and praying over the texts of Scripture.

The final paragraphs of *Dei Verbum* dreamed of a people of God committed to living by the Holy Bible in every sector of their lives (DV 21–26). The council yearned for the whole church to be renewed spiritually through the Scriptures and to become much more biblical in all aspects of her existence. Martini lived and breathed that teaching.

His mulling over the Bible in daily life retrieved the practice of *lectio divina* with which Origen and the Benedictine tradition had permanently enriched the whole church. Without using that precise term, *Dei Verbum* inculcated the practice of *lectio divina*, which was eventually named as such in the Decree on the Ministry and Life of Priests (*Presbyterorum Ordinis*).[4]

A Spirituality for Priests, Prophets, and Kings

In his hymn "Songs of Thankfulness and Praise," Christopher Wordsworth recalls how Christ at his baptism was made "manifest" as "prophet, priest, and king supreme." Through our baptism we come to share in the priestly, prophetical, and kingly or pastoral functions of our Savior. John Newton, the author of the hymn "Amazing Grace," understood this new dignity and the precious relationship it initiated as something that should be set alongside other titles of Christ and take over "my" existence. In the fourth verse of his hymn, "How Sweet the Name of Jesus Sounds,"

---

[4] See Gerald O'Collins, Appendix I: "The History and Practice of *Lectio Divina*," in *The Spiritual Exercises of St. Ignatius of Loyola: A Lived Experience* (Mahwah, NJ: Paulist Press, 2023), 145–53, at 149. See also PO 18–19.

Newman wrote, "Jesus! My Shepherd, Husband, Friend, / My Prophet, Priest, and King: / My Lord, my Life, my Way, my End, / Accept the praise I bring."

Vatican II normally avoids repeating itself. But the massive significance of sharing in Christ's priestly, prophetical, and pastoral work is underlined by repetition. Six out of sixteen of the council's documents offer teaching on those three aspects of Christ's work. Through being baptized, all the faithful take on that activity. The Decree on the Apostolate of Lay People (*Apostolicam Actuositatem*) puts matters this way: "Sharing in the function of Christ, priest, prophet, and king, the laity have an active part of their own in the life and activity of the church" (AA 10). Through their ordination, bishops, priests, and deacons accept a special way of exercising the threefold ministry. The Decree on Ecumenism (*Unitatis Redintegratio*) observes, "It is through the faithful preaching of the Gospel by . . . the bishops with Peter's successor at their head [prophetic role], through their administering the sacraments [priestly role], and through their governing in love [pastoral role], that Jesus Christ wishes his people to increase, under the action of the holy Spirit" (UR 2).

Nothing serves as well to maintain the spiritual lives of the baptized faithful than their deep sense of carrying through the priestly, prophetic, and pastoral work of our loving Savior. That conviction offers an enduring shape for their spirituality. It was implied by Pope St. John Paul II when he declared, "The greatest day of my life was the day of my baptism."[5]

Be Committed to Those in Need

In the New Testament and the works of early Christian writers, *leitourgia* (liturgy) referred both to worship and

---

[5] George Weigel, "The Most Important Day of Your Life," *Catholic Report*, April 27, 2016.

the obligation of meeting the material needs of others. The double usage of this term suggests the essential bond between worship and social action. Serving the suffering is a further, essential theme of Vatican II spirituality.[6]

Those whom Jesus expected his followers to help included the hungry, the thirsty, strangers, the naked, the sick, and prisoners (Matt 25:31–46). This list of needy people with whom Jesus identified himself did not explicitly include a typical Old Testament pair of suffering people—widows and orphans—but the list was obviously open-ended. Christ's parable of the Good Samaritan powerfully illustrated what he wanted from all his followers: the willingness to help any human being in distress (Luke 10:30–37). The words of Jesus from Matthew 25 and Luke 10, along with his parable about the Rich Man and the Poor Lazarus (Luke 16:19–31) have influenced and disturbed the conscience of Christians through the centuries, down to Vatican II and beyond.

Commitment to the needy emerges repeatedly as an essential responsibility for all Christians. Thus, the Declaration on Christian Education (*Gravissimum Educationis*) "earnestly exhorts the pastors of the church and all the faithful to spare no sacrifice in helping Catholic schools" and "in caring for the poor, for those who are without family ties, and for non-believers" (GE 9). In an eloquent passage, *Apostolicam Actuositatem* recalled the link the early church made between the Eucharist and serving the needs of suffering people, stating, "Charitable action today can

---

[6] In 2013 the original bronze statue of *Homeless Jesus* by Timothy Schmalz was installed on the campus of Regis College (Toronto). It depicts Jesus as a homeless person, still marked by the signs of the passion and sleeping on a park bench. By 2016 over one hundred copies were to be found around the world. At times, the choice of place suggests the connection between the "liturgy" of the worshipping community and its commitment to the needy. This is the case, for instance, at Newman College, University of Melbourne, where the Homeless Jesus is found right outside the entrance of the Chapel of the Holy Spirit.

and should reach all women and men and all needs" (AA 8).

Naturally *Gaudium et Spes* vividly pressed home this theme. Reclaiming Christ's story about the rich man who ignored Lazarus, it spoke of "an inescapable duty to make ourselves the neighbor of every individual, without exception, and to take positive steps to help a neighbor whom we encounter, whether that neighbor be an elderly person abandoned by everyone, a foreign worker who suffers the injustice of being despised . . . or a starving human being." The passage ended by citing the words of Christ (Matt 25:40): "As you did it to one of the least of these my brothers or sisters, you did it to me" (GS 27). Later in the same document, the council asked not only individuals but also governments to remember a classical saying: "Feed the people dying of hunger, because if you do not feed them, you are killing them" (GS 69).

Since Vatican II closed in 1965, Catholics and other Christians have grown in their conscience about the needs of our common home, the Earth. Wildfires, floods, melting ice, and air and water pollution are steadily harming our planet, impoverishing, and even extinguishing its life. If we do not actively engage ourselves in saving our Earth, we are letting it be killed.

Be Penitent Reformers

The Gospel of Mark, right at the start, pictures Christ calling on his audience to "repent and believe in the gospel" (Mark 1:15). Sincere, humble sorrow for one's sinfulness makes it possible to believe and continue to believe in Jesus, who is in person *the* good news come from God. Vatican II's Decree on Ecumenism expressed collectively this call to repentance and personal reformation: "Christ summons the church . . . to that continual reformation of which she always has need" (UR 6). Like the church herself, individual Christians remain always simultaneously sinful and holy—a description vividly and fully exemplified by what St. Paul wrote in his First Letter to the Corinthians. The spirituality of Vatican II, like any authentic Christian spirituality, incorporates repentance for sins.

The extended confession of sins at the Eucharist celebrated in St. Peter's Basilica on March 12, 2000, dramatized this picture of the church. Seven representatives of the Roman Curia gathered around a statue of Christ Crucified asking pardon for their past and present sins. Specifically, they mentioned failing to respect women and the proper freedom of conscience of all human beings.

Later in the same Jubilee Year of 2000, the drawings created by Sandro Botticelli to illustrate Dante's *Divine Comedy* were exhibited in the old papal stables in Rome. The drawings suggested a vision of the church that is simultaneously holy and sinful. The illustration for Canto 32 of the *Purgatorio*, for instance, juxtaposes (a) virtues that hold candlesticks, the four Gospel writers, a healthy young tree, the beautiful Beatrice, and the chariot of the church moving through history with (b) some monstrous outgrowths and a prostitute being courted by an ugly giant. By setting monstrosities alongside a vividly healthy group ascending into heaven, Botticelli powerfully conveyed a sense of the earthly church being both sinful and holy and needing constant reformation.

Devotion to Our Lady and Other Saints

The Dogmatic Constitution on the Church dedicated an entire chapter to the Blessed Virgin Mary (LG 52–69). *Lumen Gentium* also encouraged Catholics and other Christians to venerate, imitate, and invoke the intercession of the saints in heaven (LG 51). A spirituality drawn from Vatican II embodies devotion to Our Lady and the other saints. Let me concentrate on devotion to the Virgin Mary.

Previous general councils of the church—for instance, the

Council of Ephesus—had taught significant things about the Virgin Mary. But Vatican II was the first such council to treat extensively the figure of Mary and devotion to her. It placed that teaching within the two-thousand-year-old life and tradition of the entire church. Art, prayer, and music express that long tradition.

A visit to the Basilica of St. Mary Major in Rome leaves the deepest impression on some pilgrims and not least through the history of devotion to Mary that it incorporates. In the square outside, a fluted column, which came from a fourth-century building constructed by Emperor Constantine, supports a seventeenth-century statue of the Virgin Mary. Completed in AD 440, the basilica itself contains the first figures ever made for a Christmas crib, the figures of the Christ Child, Mary, and the others created by Arnolfo di Cambio and his assistants (late thirteenth century). A twelfth-century mosaic represents the Virgin Mary sitting on a throne beside her divine Son. It recalls how the Council of Ephesus in AD 431 upheld her already popular title of *Theotokos* or Mother of God. She conceived, gave birth to, and mothered the Son of God and the Savior of the world (see LG 66).

Chartres Cathedral (begun AD 1145) also classically displays what following Jesus and devotion to his Mother should mean. The rich sculpture, stained glass, and luminous structure of this Gothic cathedral have always inspired superlatives. A descendant of two American presidents, Henry Adams (1838–1918), wrote in *Mont-Saint-Michel and Chartres*: "If you want to know what churches were made for, come down here on some great festival of the Virgin, and give yourself up to it; but come alone! That kind of knowledge cannot be taught and can seldom be shared."[7]

Prayers like the *Memorare* and the Rosary—along

---

[7] Henry Adams, *Mont-Saint-Michel and Chartres* (Boston: Houghton Mifflin Company, 1913), 108.

with the *Salve Regina*, the *Regina Coeli*, and other Marian antiphons—witness to the love for Our Lady that has characterized all authentic Christian spirituality. The most celebrated setting for the *Magnificat* is arguably one by Johann Sebastian Bach. Such music conveys best of all that Vatican II summarized in prose: the enduring place of Mary in Catholic Christianity. The *Akathistos*, an ancient song of praise to the Mother of God, does the same for Eastern Christians, Catholic and Orthodox.

Be in Dialogue with Everyone

Much of what has been said so far characterizes the spirituality of Vatican II. Yet many other spiritualities encourage the Christian faithful to be centered on Jesus, immersed in the inspired Scriptures, and so forth. Far from being exclusive, such themes regularly describe Christian spiritualities. The council can strike fresh, distinctive notes for spiritual practice—not least by the invitation to be in dialogue with every human being.

Vatican II ended its last and longest document, *Gaudium et Spes*, with an attractive plea that fits the scope of that text: "All who constitute the one people of God" should "engage in ever more fruitful dialogue, whether they are pastors or other members of the faithful" (GS 92). This Pastoral (read spiritual) Constitution on the Church in the Modern World gracefully proposed three circles of dialogue: within the Catholic Church, with other Christians, and with all others, whatever their religious faith or lack of it.

The council itself had not only followed the example and advice of Pope St. Paul VI but also set a fine example of such dialogue in practice. Think, for instance, of the Declaration on Relations of the Church to Non-Christian Religions (*Nostra Aetate*) and the Decree on Ecumenism (*Unitatis Redintegratio*).

The practice of Christian dialogue means nothing less

than taking the Holy Trinity as the supreme role model. The life of the Trinity is essentially dialogical. As Cardinal Walter Kasper has written, "The divine persons are not less dialogical but infinitely more dialogical than human beings are. The divine persons are not only in dialogue, they *are* dialogue."[8]

Conclusion

My eight invitations from Vatican II, when taken together, can shape the systematic practice of a Christian spiritual life: be centered on Jesus and his manifold presence; be actively liturgical; be constantly shaped by the Bible; be priestly, prophetic, and pastoral; be generously committed to all in need, including a planet in need; live like a repentant sinner; be devoted to Our Lady and the saints; and be in dialogue with everyone. If we recall and put into practice these invitations, we will live by a spirituality shaped by the meaning and message of Vatican II.

Every blessing to all my readers. I pray and hope that this year be filled for you with the grace and peace that can come to us through the teaching of Vatican II and not least its spirituality.

[8] Walter Kasper, *The God of Jesus Christ*, trans. Matthew J. O'Connell (New York: Crossroad, 1984), 290 (emphasis in original).

10

Synodality

An Enduring Legacy of the Council

Robert W. McElroy

Pope Francis has called the whole of the church to a profound process of renewal through a synodal process that seeks to touch and transform every element of our ecclesial life and our outreach to the world. The theme of synodality has been at the heart of this pontificate, and Francis has identified it as a constitutive dimension of the church's charter and life. Indeed, the pope has stated that "it is precisely this path of *synodality* [emphasis in original] which God expects of the Church of the third millennium."[1]

The scope and nature of this call to reform and renewal is reflected in Francis's explanation that the synodal process is, by its very nature, an effort to "plant dreams, draw forth prophecies and visions, allow hope to flourish, inspire trust, bind up wounds, weave together relationships, awaken a

[1] Francis, Ceremony Commemorating the 50th Anniversary of the Institution of the Synod of Bishops, October 17, 2015.

dawn of hope, learn from one another, and create a bright resourcefulness that will enlighten minds, warm hearts, give strength to our hands."[2]

It is also in the most fundamental sense a call to conversion to the whole church, recognizing that the current synodal process seeks an outcome far beyond the issuance of new documents, or even a moment of change, but rather an ongoing process of reform and renewal that constantly enhances ecclesial life from the parish to the diocese to the world church.

As we seek to assess the current state of the synodal challenge in our country, it is helpful to analyze three issues. The first of these is the history of synodality in the life of the church and the role of the Second Vatican Council in recovering the synodal tradition and propelling it forward in the life of the church. The second is the distinctive architecture of Francis's specific call to synodality and how that builds upon the work of the council. And the third is the synodal witness that the church in the United States has given during the past year.

Synodality in the Life and History of the Church

The International Theological Commission states that the Greek word *synod*, or journeying together, "is an ancient and venerable word in the Tradition of the Church, whose meaning draws on the deepest themes of Revelation. . . . It indicates the path along which the People of God walk together. Equally, it refers to the Lord Jesus, who presents Himself as 'the way, the truth, and the life' (Jn 14:6), and to the fact that Christians, His followers, were originally called 'followers of

[2] Francis, The Opening of the Synod of Bishops on Young People, the Faith, and Vocational Discernment, October 3, 2018.

the way' (cf. Acts 9:2; 19:9–23; 22:4; 24:14–22)."[3]

Particularly important in understanding the history of synodality in the life of the early church is the Council of Jerusalem, for in this moment one can discern the synodal pathway coming into being. The church in Jerusalem meets to discuss the proper response to the pastoral issues which have been brought to them by the community of Antioch. It is the apostles and the elders who are consulted in this first instance, but it is the entire church of Jerusalem that participates in the synodal action of discerning the light of the Gospel and the guidance of the Holy Spirit.

Ever since the first century, the term "synod" has been used for the ecclesial gatherings convened at diocesan, regional, or universal levels, to discern where God was calling the church to move on doctrinal, pastoral, and liturgical issues. In diocesan synods, the whole community by tradition took part in the discernment. In the regional and ecumenical synods, bishops were the central participants in union. The Preparatory Document for the current synod clarifies this legacy: "In the first millennium, 'journeying together'—that is, practicing synodality—was the ordinary way in which the Church, understood as 'People united in the unity of the Father and of the Son and of the Holy Spirit,' acted. To those who were creating division in the ecclesial body, the Church Fathers opposed the communion of Churches scattered throughout the world, described by St. Augustine as '*concordissima fidei conspiratio*,' that is, the agreement of faith of all of the Baptized."[4] Indeed, St. John Chrysostom stated that "church and synod are synonymous."[5]

---

[3] International Theological Commission, "Synodality in the Life and Mission of the Church," March 2, 2018, no. 3.

[4] Synod of Bishops, The Preparatory Document, September 7, 2021, no. 11.

[5] "*ekklēssia gar systēmatos kai synodou estin onoma,*" in St. John

The synodal focus of the church in the first millennium was rooted in a rich theology of *communio*. This concept proceeds from the unity of the Father, Son, and Spirit that should be reflected in the life of the church. It embraces the conviction that the one baptism of all believers and the sharing of the Eucharist create a bond among the local churches even as they may differ in many specific practices. *Communio* is realized in the participation of all the local churches in discerning God's will and manifesting grace in the life of the universal Christian community.

Pope Francis has made *communio* a key pillar in his theology of synodality. Here is how it is framed in his call to the present synodal moment:

> By his gracious will, God gathers us together as diverse peoples of one faith, through the covenant that he offers to his people. The communion we share finds its deepest roots in the love and unity of the Trinity. It is Christ who reconciles us to the Father and unites us with each other in the Holy Spirit. Together, we are inspired by listening to the Word of God, through the living Tradition of the Church, and grounded in the *sensus fidei* that we share. We all have a role to play in discerning and living out God's call for his people.[6]

Following the split of AD 1054, in the Western church the hierarchical dimensions of the church's identity received ever greater prominence in tandem with an escalating focus on the papacy. In contrast, in the Eastern church, the concept

---

Chrysostom, "Explanation of Psalm 149," in *Patrologia Graeca* 55.493; see also The Preparatory Document, no. 11.

[6] Francis, For a Synodal Church: Communion, Participation, and Mission, Vademecum for the Synod on Synodality, September 7, 2021, no. 1.4.

of synod and its collegial stress on *communio*, listening, and consensus remained strong.

Vatican II did not utilize the term "synodality." But as the International Theological Commission has noted, "Synodality is at the heart of the work of renewal the Council was encouraging. The ecclesiology of the People of God stresses the common dignity and mission of all the baptized, in exercising the variety and ordered richness of their charisms, their vocations and their ministries. . . . In this ecclesiological context, synodality is the specific *modus vivendi et operandi* of the Church, the People of God, which reveals and gives substance to her being as communion when all of her members journey together, gather in assembly, and take an active part in her evangelizing mission."[7] This conciliar focus upon the entire people of God generated mandates for local structures of participation in the wake of the council: presbyteral councils, diocesan pastoral councils, and parish finance councils. The council also gave rise to the recovery of the synodal tradition of collegiality among bishops in its theology and in the specific structure of the formal synods of bishops that have taken place to discuss central questions that the church has faced during the past fifty years. Hence, in pointing to the concept of synodality as the pathway God is calling the church to follow in the third millennium, Pope Francis is, on a critically important level, calling for a moment of rediscovery of the church's history and identity.

That is why the term "synodality" is not optional in our process of reform as a church. It embodies vital elements of the ecclesial life that Vatican II called us to in this moment of history: the pilgrim nature of the church, the need for

---

[7] International Theological Commission, "Synodality in the Life and Mission of the Church," no. 6.

communio, the effective realization of structures that are both hierarchical and embrace the entire people of God, and the pivotal guidance of the Holy Spirit. The concept of synodality reminds us that those same elements have always been crucial to the church's historic mission as the pilgrim people of God, journeying together in the light of the Gospel of Jesus Christ.

A Moment of Doctrinal Development

If Pope Francis is drawing clearly upon the historic tradition of synodality in the life of the church, it is crucial to recognize that he has also been engaged in the process of doctrinal development regarding synodality throughout his pontificate. Strikingly, Francis utilizes the term "synodality," which had not itself been used historically in the life of the church. This term, as the International Theological Commission has noted, "is a sign of something new that has been maturing in the ecclesial consciousness starting from the Magisterium of Vatican II, and from the lived experience of local Churches and the universal Church since the last Council until today."[8]

It is crucial to recognize that the contribution that Pope Francis is making to the historic notion of synod in the life of the church is not primarily a linguistic one. Rather, Francis is drawing upon the tradition of synod in the light of the lived realities of the postconciliar church to delineate a specific architecture of synodality for this current moment in our history. This process is one of reclamation, refinement, and transformation. It speaks to the core of ecclesial life, and not just to peripheral issues. It presents synodality as a process of conversion, recognizing that the renewal it demands is not possible within a short time frame. It represents a con-

[8] International Theological Commission, "Synodality in the Life and Mission of the Church," no. 5.

tinuing call to reform within the life of the church. Most of all, it proposes that discernment for the pilgrim people of God must reach into every level of the universal church and invite all people into meaningful participation.

Precisely because the theology of synodality that Pope Francis is presenting to the global church has a specific architecture and content, it is vital to understand the pivotal distinguishing marks that characterize Pope Francis's vision of a synodal church and any synodal process.

First, synodality points to the reality that the whole of the people of God is journeying together in the life of the church and in synodal action. This means that we cannot operate from a mind-set of complacency or one that accentuates the differences among the baptized. Rather, we must follow the example of the people of Israel in the desert who were united in their faith and in their understanding that God was calling them to an ever-new way of life that would be filled with many unexpected elements, some welcome and some not. The central conciliar image for the church as the pilgrim people of God is the soul of synodality.

Second, synodality demands a constant stance of discernment; that is, a stance of seeking the guidance of the Holy Spirit within the life of the community. It is all too easy for us in ecclesial life at all levels to become focused on the perspectives that we bring to dialogue and decision-making, instead of first submerging our perspectives, interests, and alignments to listening to the small, whispering sound that Elijah recognized as the voice of God calling to him (1 Kgs 19:11–13).

Third, synodality entails a penetrating call to conversion and change. The greatest contribution that St. Augustine's *Confessions* made to the life of the church was its central recognition that the call to conversion to us as individual believers, as parishioners, and as participants in the life of the world is a call that never ends and is never easy. We all tend to become set in our ways in a manner that limits our ability to authentically grow as disciples of Jesus Christ. Synodality calls us to overcome our complacency and remain actively engaged in the process of lifelong change that lies at the heart of discipleship for us as individuals and as participants in the life of the church. This call to holiness and unity is one of the great recovered emphases in our faith that the council underscored.

Fourth, synodality is continually rooted in listening to the word of God and celebrating the Eucharist, which is, in the words of the council, the "source and summit" of the Christian life (LG 11; SC 10). These elements are both constitutive realities that form the church and vital nourishment for the community as a whole. Synodality demands a deeply celebrative understanding of the life in the church that proceeds from word and sacrament and embraces the building of community in the church at all levels through diverse cultural, interpersonal, prayerful, and structural forms. The revolution in the Catholic understanding of the word of God that took place in the council has become a powerful new foundation for both ecclesial and personal discipleship. And the joy of basking in the overwhelming gift of the resurrection of Jesus Christ should continually animate this celebrative dimension of the church's life.

Fifth, synodality demands a profound stance of authentic listening from every believer who seeks to participate in and contribute to the life of the church. The Scriptures tell us that God listens attentively to the cry of God's people. Listening is the respect we owe to others in recognition of their equal dignity. Listening flows from a recognition that we have so much to learn. Listening lies at the heart of true encounter with the other disciples we meet in the life of the church, yet a stance of authentic listening is hard to embrace and sustain. It can be frustrating, and it is always demanding. But it is the only pathway through which others can, without fear, truly open their hearts, and through which we can genuinely open our hearts to others. Vatican

II was a journey in respectful listening and dialogue. It was a journey that millions of Catholics throughout the world accompanied raptly. And it was the first ecclesial moment in which the people of God could truly participate.

Sixth, a synodal church is a humble and honest church. Such a church acknowledges and seeks to atone for the wounds it has brought to others, particularly the sexual abuse of young people. It seeks to shatter the culture of clericalism that has wrought grievous harm by distorting the beautiful gift of priesthood into a possession or a caste, with all the sinfulness that such a sense of privilege brings with it. A synodal church genuinely seeks to discern its woundedness and embrace reform. Its holiness is exemplified by its humility, not by denial or the protection of its reputation. The council was an invitation to a humbler church on many levels—rejecting the theology of the "perfect society" in favor of that of a pilgrim people (LG 48–51) or sacrament (LG 1), or servant. Yet the council did not go far enough in confronting the sinful structures and cultures that lay within it. It is important that the synodal process take up the process that the council began.

Seventh, a synodal church is a discerning church, not a parliamentary one. It must empower the voices of all, but its search for God's will cannot be reduced to building majorities or forming coalitions. It is essential to recognize that synodality is more concerned with nurturing a culture within the life of the church rather than specific policy outcomes. It recognizes the important hierarchical dimensions of our ecclesial life and tradition and finds its foundation in the equal dignity of all the baptized. Synodality refuses to be governed by the delusion of self-sufficiency or ideological frameworks that obscure the realities of our lives and our world.

Eighth, a synodal church seeks a healthy decentralization in its structures and life. At the very heart of synodality lies the heritage of the church of the first millennium that embodied genuine *communio* through emphasizing collegial participation of the bishops, either regionally or universally, in addressing questions of faith, worship, and practice. The heritage of synod in the early church also pointed to the integral office of bishop of the local church as a constitutive dimension of the church, not a derivative or deputized one. As Vatican II proclaimed, the bishop is the shepherd of the local church, not in a manner of delegation from the pope, but as a direct sacramental and pastoral reality that lies in the structure of the church itself. The preeminence and jurisdiction of the bishop of Rome must be fully recognized in any actions and structures that seek to embody collegiality. But a true principle of subsidiarity is critical for the building of a synodal church.

Ninth, synodality demands a participative, inclusive, and co-responsible church. Such a synodal vision integrates the historic structure of the church, the pivotal role of the college of bishops, and the ministry of unity and continuity that the pope provides. At the same time, it calls lay men and women to expanded roles in the breadth of the church's ministries and apostolates. The seeds planted by the council must continue to be nurtured in our midst if the ecclesial vision of the council is to be vindicated.

The Synodal Dialogues

In 2021–2022, the Catholic community in the United States undertook the largest process of interpersonal dialogue and consultation ever held in our nation's history. More than five hundred thousand men and women gathered together in prayer and discernment in their parishes, schools, cultural communities, and service organizations to share their joys and their sorrows, their hopes, and their fears touching upon the life of the church.

One of the most striking realities reflected in our national dialogues was the commonality of the perceptions and questions of the people of God across dioceses, regions, and cultures within our country. While sometimes framed in different languages or with different emphases, the joys, the hopes, the sorrows, and the fears of God's people were remarkably similar. For this reason, it is truly possible to see in the results of the dialogue a composite picture of the Catholic community in the United States today, and a picture of where we must move in the years to come. There are seven elements of this picture that are of central importance.

First, *the synodal dialogues were a moment of tremendous growth for so many participants, because they revealed the power of listening to others, placing oneself totally at their disposal to share their experiences, joys, and pains*. As the church of the Midwest testified, "The value of simply listening is a clear message of the Synod process. People must be able to speak honestly on even the most controversial topics without fear of rejection. We must be open to new ideas and new ways of doing things. That will require an understanding of what is central to the identity of the church, diocese, and parish; and what changes can help us grow rather than feel threatened."[9] What a clear manifestation of the culture of dialogue and respect the council has unleashed in the global church. The Diocese of Fresno noted that, because of the dialogue experience, there "was the sense of gratitude for the safe space that was created to share thoughts, opinions, hopes, disappointments, and sorrows, without judgment or prejudice, even when thoughts conflicted or were the opposite of someone else's."[10]

---

[9] USCCB, "National Synthesis of the People of God in the United States of America for the Diocesan Phase of the 2021–2023 Synod," 12, https://www.usccb.org/resources/US%20National%20Synthesis%202021-2023%20Synod.pdf.

[10] USCCB, "Synodal Synthesis Document (Region XI—California and Nevada—USA)," no. II, 2, https://www.usccb.org/resources/Region%20XI%20Synthesis%20Final.pdf.

Second, *community lies at the heart of the church*. People spoke lovingly of the webs of faith, friendship, searching, love, compassion, justice, and hope that have enriched their lives in the communities of the church. These include a vast array of prayer and formation groups, liturgical ministries, outreach to the sick and the marginalized, schools, cultural communities, and social activities that truly give shape to the Body of Christ in our nation. The Catholic community is journeying together because its vibrant and disparate communities of children and families rejoice together, mourn together, question together, grow together, and find a home, all within a framework of faith.

Yet even as the synodal call to journey together highlighted the beautiful bonds of friendship and community that exist within the church, it also accented the polarization that is a cancer in our church in the present day. One dialogue participant observed sadly, "The divisive political ideologies present in our society have seeped into all aspects of our lives."[11] Another lamented that "people at both ends of the political spectrum have set up camp opposing the 'others,' forgetting that they are one in the Body of Christ."[12] It was noted widely in the dialogues that there was no unity among the bishops on key questions of pastoral life and mission in the world. This is a scandal of division that is deeply dispiriting to the laity, and indeed to the whole of the church.

Third, *the synodal dialogues testified emphatically to the power of the Eucharist in the lives of believers*. As the Diocese of San Diego noted in its synthesis, "The principal joy that emerged in the synodal sessions was participation in the sacramental life of the Church. The declaration of one participant that 'experiencing the beauty of our Church/Mass with our families is what brings us hope' was emblem-

---

[11] USCCB, "National Synthesis," 5.

[12] USCCB, "National Synthesis," 5.

atic of comments in virtually every small group sharing."[13]

The vast majority of synod participants pointed to the sacramental life of the church as the richest source for sustenance and growth in their spiritual lives. They expressed great gratitude to their priests for the sacrificial, prayerful, and caring love that they bring to the sacramental life of the church as celebrant of the Eucharist and in bringing the sacraments to those in desperate need. What we witness here is the fruit of the renewal of the eucharistic theology and sacramental life accomplished at the council and in the years following it. It is in the full and active participation of our people in the Eucharist and the sacramental life of the church that the work of the council shines with God's grace in the individual and communal life of Catholics.

Fourth, *the issue of sexual abuse surfaced in virtually every dialogue*. One of the strongest themes of the synodal dialogues throughout the country was anger at the way in which bishops knowingly reassigned priests whom they knew had sexually abused minors. The strength and starkness with which this anger against our nation's bishops endures in the life of the church is revealed in the comments of the national synthesis of the local dialogues: "Trust in the hierarchy of the Church is weak and needs to be strengthened. The sex abuse scandals and the way the Church leadership handled the situation are seen as one of the strongest causes of a lack of trust and credibility on the part of the faithful. Feedback revealed the strong, lingering wound caused by the abuse of power and the physical, emotional, and spiritual abuse of the most innocent in our community."[14]

Fifth, *the call to the church fostering an inclusive com-*

---

[13] Diocese of San Diego, "Synthesis—the Synodal Process," June 2022, 4, https://sdcatholic.org/wp-content/uploads/synod/2022-reports/Synod_ProcessReport_A_Eng.pdf.

[14] USCCB, "National Synthesis," 5.

munity was one of the most predominant themes throughout the listening sessions. Our national tapestry of marginalization in the church was captured in the testimony of the church in Los Angeles: "The divorced long for participation in communal life. Likewise, the divorced and remarried yearn to return to sacramental life but feel the annulment processes are too burdensome. Individuals without housing or jobs, recent immigrants, the elderly, those with disabilities, those suffering from alcoholism, drug addiction and mental health issues, and the incarcerated and their families also live on the margins of our parish communities. At times, lesbian, gay, bisexual, and transgender individuals and their loved ones experience judgment and rejection, and are confused and hurt by the harsh words and actions of some Church leaders."[15]

This searing question of the church's treatment of LGBTQ+ persons was an immensely prominent facet of the synodal dialogues. Anguished voices within the LGBTQ+ communities, in unison with their families, cried out against the perception that they are condemned by the church and individual Catholics in a devastating way. One parish community desperately sought help: "There is an urgent need for guidance. . . . 'We believe we are approaching a real crisis in how to minister to the LGBTQ+ community, some of whom are members of our own families. We need help, support, and clarity.' "[16] Faith-filled parents of LGBTQ+ children were especially vocal in their call for greater inclusion from the church, as were young adults. It is clear that the church in the United States must transform its outreach

---

[15] Archdiocese of Los Angeles, "Synod 2021–2023 Report—Diocesan Synthesis Submission," 3, https://synod.lacatholics.org/documents/2022/9/ADLA%20Diocesan%20Synthesis%20Submission.pdf.

[16] USCCB, "National Synthesis," 8.

to LGBTQ+ persons if it seeks to be a truly welcoming presence in the world.

The church of the Northwest pointed to another facet of marginalization in the reality that "Catholic people of color spoke of routine encounters with racism, both inside and outside the Church. Indigenous Catholics spoke of the generational trauma caused by racism and abuse in boarding schools."[17]

The issue of women constituted a central focus of critique in the national dialogues. The Diocese of Las Vegas concluded that "as regards the role of women, a small minority of respondents voiced the opinion that women should be excluded from any liturgical or ministerial roles. . . . The vast majority of respondents, however, strongly opposed this attitude and urged Church leaders to recognize the '*unique charisms*' and '*pastoral gifts*' [emphasis in original] women bring to the Church. Broad support for ordaining women was voiced by those participating in the synodal process as were calls to include women in leadership positions, discussions, and decisions on all levels of the Church."[18] The strength with which all of these ideas were expressed across every region in the country points to the enduring failures of the church to engage and treat women in the manner in which justice demands.

This exclusion of women in the church is part of a wider reality in which lay Catholics are often marginalized in important ways in the life of the church. Addressing this issue requires two elements. The first is the recognition that lay women and men have both the talents and the right to

---

[17] USCCB, "National Synthesis," 9.

[18] Diocese of Las Vegas, "Synthesis Submission," June 2022, 4, https://files.ecatholic.com/32314/documents/2022/10/FINAL%20Diocese%20of%20Las%20Vegas%20Synthesis%20for%20Website.pdf?t=1666026787000.

leadership roles in their parishes, dioceses, and communities. The church in Iowa, Kansas, Missouri, and Nebraska spoke directly to this reality: "Many want to see Church leadership take more seriously the talents and knowledge of the laity. Some expressed the need to use more effective Parish Councils and Diocesan Pastoral Councils. Others want their pastors and bishops to explore more deeply with the laity how best to participate in understanding the mission of the Church and its efforts to evangelize its members and the world."[19] These are the conciliar signs of the times that cry out to us for reform and renewal in the present day.

Sixth, *the synodal witness continually expressed profound gratitude to priests for their devoted service to the church and the sacrifices that they make.* As the people of the Diocese of Brownsville witnessed, "An overwhelming majority of the synodal consultations affirmed a love and appreciation for parish priests. Many parishioners shared the impact of the pastor's personal invitation and encouragement. They recounted examples of difficult times, moments of celebration, and of active life and service in the Church. Many had profound experiences with their pastor in the sacrament of confession, the celebration of the Holy Mass, and funerals."[20]

At the same time, the corrosive elements of clerical culture frequently erect a chasm between priests and bishops and their people. It surfaces in priests or bishops who do not see in their own limits the invitation to more collaborative relationships, not less. It surfaces when priesthood becomes a possession, a status rather than an invitation to servant leadership. It appears in the actions of those who confuse

---

[19] USCCB, "National Synthesis," 11.

[20] Diocese of Brownsville, "Synthesis of Diocesan Phase Consultations," June 30, 2022, 9, https://files.ecatholic.com/30330/documents/2022/9/EN%20CDOB%20SYNOD%20SYNTHESIS%20Sep%202%202022%20final.pdf?t=1663163694000.

having the final decision-making role in a parish or diocese with having no other vigorous alternative opinions, voices, and ideas. These realities testify that we have far to go in replacing the image of priesthood as *alter Christus* with the conciliar image of servant leader. And on many levels, it seems that we in the church in the United States are going in reverse.

Seventh, *perhaps the greatest missionary challenge that emerged during the synodal dialogues was the need to invite our young adults back into the life of the church.* The National Synthesis observes, "Practically all synodal consultations shared a deep ache in the wake of the departure of young people and viewed this as integrally connected to becoming a more welcoming Church."[21] The church in New Jersey and Pennsylvania said, "Youth who participated in synodal sessions . . . stressed that they should not be seen and spoken of mostly as the future of the Church, but should be recognized for their importance now and given a significant voice in the present. They want to be both seen and heard and included more in Church life, especially by participating meaningfully in parish and diocesan councils and ministries."[22] Young adults often spoke of feeling as foreigners in the church in which they grew up. There were many calls for the church to speak out about issues of particular interest to young adults, such as justice, race, and climate change.

The weight of this existential imperative was reflected in the enormous suffering that tens of thousands of parents expressed over their children's alienation from the church. One parent said, "I feel like a failure because I was not able to hand down my faith to my children who are now adults."[23] Another lamented, "It breaks our hearts to see

---

[21] USCCB, "National Synthesis," 9.
[22] USCCB, "National Synthesis," 9.
[23] USCCB, "National Synthesis," 9.

our children that we brought to Mass and sent to Catholic schools and colleges reject the Church."[24]

Eighth, *one key element of synodality that was so prominent in the life of the council, but largely ignored in the local dialogues, was outreach to the world. This includes both a lack of focus on the role of Catholic social teaching in transforming the world, and a more general inattention to the missionary outreach to the wider world in spreading the Gospel of Jesus Christ in a sustained and comprehensive manner.* Father Lou Cameli pointed to this reality in an article he wrote for *America* magazine. After reviewing the dialogue summaries from the Archdiocese of Chicago, he says, a deficit "I found in the responses was something Pope Francis has called 'ecclesial introversion,' a sticky attachment to the internal life of the church and its structural-institutional organization. The whole point of synodality is to be 'on the road together' in mission, going outside of ourselves. So many comments in the responses spoke to recommend changes in church life or, even more accurately, *within* [emphasis in original] church life. The sense of outward mission was generally faint. Formation for mission, an ever-expansive sense of our purpose in the world, needs to take hold of our communities of faith."[25] This may be the most significant challenge to synodality that has surfaced in the local dialogues.

Conclusion

Without Vatican II, synodality would never have been reborn in our age. The ecclesial vision, the effort to make the liturgical life of the church participative rather than

---

[24] USCCB, "National Synthesis," 9.

[25] Louis J. Cameli, "I Reviewed All of My Diocese's Synod Responses: Their Missing Elements Could Point the Way Forward for the Church," *America*, August 18, 2022.

passive, the notion that dialogue and accompaniment are constitutive dimensions of the church, the move toward decentralization in church structures, and the willingness to see and present the church in a humbler stance were all pivotal to bringing our world church to this present moment of renewal and reform. May the church of this moment reflect the same vision and energy and openness that were present in Rome sixty years ago.